Communicating Effectively

Other titles in the Briefcase Books Series include:

To learn more about titles in the Briefcase Books series go to **www.briefcasebooks.com**

You'll find the tables of contents, downloadable sample chapters, information on the authors, discussion guides for using these books in training programs, and more.

Communicating Effectively

Lani Arredondo

McGraw-Hill

New York San Francisco Washington, D.C. Auckland Bogotá
Caracas Lisbon London Madrid Mexico City Milan
Montreal New Delhi San Juan Singapore
Sydney Tokyo Toronto

McGraw-Hill

A Division of The **McGraw·Hill** Companies

3 4 5 6 7 8 9 0 AGM/AGM 0 9 8 7 6 5 4 3 2 1 0

ISBN 0-07-136429-3

This is a CWL Publishing Enterprises Book, *developed and produced for McGraw-Hill by* CWL Publishing Enterprises, *John A. Woods, President. For more information, contact CWL Publishing Enterprises, 3010 Irvington Way, Madison, WI 53713-3414, www.cwlpub.com. Robert Magnan served as editor. For McGraw-Hill, the sponsoring editor is Catherine Schwent, and the publisher is Jeffrey Krames.*

Printed and bound by Quebecor/Martinsburg.

This publication is designed to provide accurate and authoritative information in regard to the subject matter covered. It is sold with the understanding that neither the author nor the publisher is engaged in rendering legal, accounting, or other professional service. If legal advice or other expert assistance is required, the services of a competent professional person should be sought.
   —*From a Declaration of Principles jointly adopted by a Committee of the American Bar Association and a Committee of Publishers*

McGraw-Hill books are available at special quantity discounts to use as premiums and sale promotions, or for use in corporate training programs. For more information, please write to the Director of Special Sales, McGraw-Hill, 2 Penn Plaza, New York, NY 10128. Or contact your local bookstore.

 This book is printed on recycled, acid-free paper containing a minimum of 50% recycled de-inked fiber.

Contents

Preface

While writing this book, I had occasion to recall many of the people I've dealt with during my career. Those who have made the most positive impression on me, and who've had the most positive influence on others as well, all share in common one quality. They're excellent communicators.

At times, I considered my interactions with others. Whether working with customers or team members, reporting to a manager or serving as one, I've enjoyed better results when I applied the skills presented in this book. It's been a reminder of the old saying, "practice what you preach."

I've also reflected on how much communications have changed. I've seen the introduction of cell phones, pagers, voice mail, e-mail, fax, video conferencing, and Internet chat rooms. Communicating has never been faster or easier. With all of these high-tech devices, we can now communicate with just about anyone, anywhere, at any time. But are we communicating any better?

Plenty of evidence suggests that often we're not. Many work groups are riddled with conflict, frequently a consequence of poor communication. Misunderstandings occur and misinformation spreads. At work and at home, relationships become strained because of negative communications. And we experience that so-called "failure to communicate." Solutions to these unnecessary problems lie in improving our ability to interact with one another constructively.

Before computerized transmissions, before electronic walkie-talkies, youngsters devised a low-tech device: two tin cans tied together by a string. As rudimentary as it is, this tin-can toy illustrates the objective of communication: to create a durable connection and keep it intact.

In this book, you'll discover how to do that. You'll learn the essentials of effective communication, refinements for specific situations, and how to build better relationships through proven interpersonal skills. Put it all together and you can be (if you aren't already) an excellent communicator yourself.

Special Features

The idea behind the books in the Briefcase Series is to give you practical information written in a friendly person-to-person style. The chapters are short, deal with tactical issues, and include lots of examples. They also feature numerous boxes designed to give you different types of specific information. Here's a description of the boxes you'll find in this book.

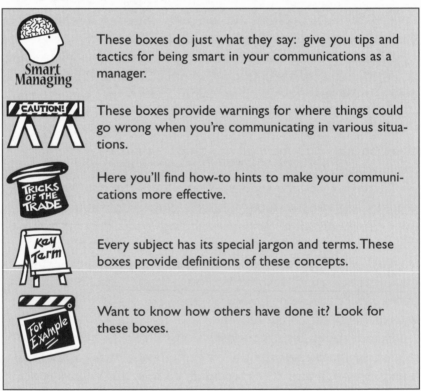

These boxes do just what they say: give you tips and tactics for being smart in your communications as a manager.

These boxes provide warnings for where things could go wrong when you're communicating in various situations.

Here you'll find how-to hints to make your communications more effective.

Every subject has its special jargon and terms. These boxes provide definitions of these concepts.

Want to know how others have done it? Look for these boxes.

Here you'll find specific procedures you can follow for special on-the-job communications situations.

How can you make sure you won't make a mistake when communicating? You can't, but these boxes will give you practical advice on how to minimize the possibility.

Acknowledgments

Thanks to John Woods of CWL Publishing Enterprises for his work in bringing this project to completion and to Bob Magnan at CWL for his editing work. To my husband, Jess, for his endless encouragement and patience. And to my colleagues who model what it means to be an effective communicator—you know who you are.

About the Author

Lani Arredondo is a trainer and conference speaker specializing in communication and management skills.

An honors graduate of the University of California, she enjoyed an award-winning career with IBM, served on the faculty of National University's School of Business and Management, and was a top-rated trainer with a leading international seminar company.

She is the author of two other books from McGraw-Hill: *How to Present Like a Pro* and *The McGraw-Hill 36-Hour Course in Business Presentations*.

It's All About Communication

You arrive for work bright and early, ready for a productive day. No sooner have you entered the building than you're accosted by an employee who has a complaint. "Well," she demands, "what are you going to do about it?" You promise to get back to her later in the day.

You head down the hall toward your office. An employee greets you cheerfully. Another glares and grumbles. "I've got to talk to him about that attitude," you think.

Stopping by the break room for coffee, you notice a few of your staff seated around a table in the corner. "What's up?" you ask pleasantly, meaning to strike up a friendly conversation. "Nothing," one of them mumbles. You surmise something is up, considering how their conversation stopped abruptly when you entered the room.

At your desk, you power on the computer to check your e-mail. The usual: 37 messages and it's only 8:15. You'll attend to them later. First, you need to check with the human resources department about getting the new hire through orientation.

As soon as you pick up the phone to call human resources, your boss appears. "Need you in a meeting at 9 about the Jones account. It'll only take fifteen minutes." You know better. These "only" meetings go on longer than that.

With less than 45 minutes until the meeting, you do a quick mental calculation. Should you jot down notes for your presentation to the staff tomorrow? Meet with Jane to give her instructions on the next project phase? Call Joe in to talk about that attitude problem you've noticed? Get together with the manager of quality control about those defects in the gizmos? Review the Jones file? Check on that employee's complaint? Reply to the e-mails, voice mails, memos, letters, faxes, ad infinitum? Brrriiing ... your telephone rings. Saved by the bell.

Nobody told you it would be like this!

What You Do

Call to mind a typical week at work. Of the activities listed below, place a checkmark next to those you do on a regular basis. Estimate, on average, the percentage of time you spend on each.

_____	Work on tasks or projects	_____%
_____	Discussions with the boss	_____%
_____	Conversations with peers	_____%
_____	Discussions with employees	_____%
_____	Give employees instructions	_____%
_____	Give employees feedback	_____%
_____	Interview	_____%
_____	Lead or take part in meetings	_____%
_____	Make presentations	_____%
_____	Compose memos, letters, e-mail	_____%
_____	Telephone calls	_____%
_____	Other activities	_____%

All of these activities involve *communicating* in one form or another. Chances are, you spend the bulk of your time involved in such activities. No matter what your "official" title—team leader, supervisor, manager, director, business owner, or the like—if you manage people, communication is a critical part of what you do.

A Model of Management

Suppose you signed up for a course entitled Management 101. During the first session, the instructor poses this question to the class: "What is management?" How would you answer the question?

Figure 1-1 suggests some answers to this question.

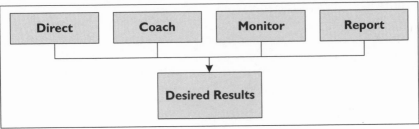

Figure 1-1. What does a manager do?

After decisions are made about the results to be accomplished in the area you manage, you direct and coach employee performance toward achieving those desired results. You then monitor what's going on and report on progress or problems.

At every stage, you *communicate*. You interact with the boss, with employees, and with other departments. You may interface with entities outside of the organization, including suppliers, contractors, and government or community agencies.

At every stage, you encounter this challenge. You're accountable for seeing that results are achieved. But you don't produce them directly yourself. The results are produced by others (unless you're a "working supervisor" doing the jobs of both employee and manager). In other words, you're in the middle of it all (Figure 1-2):

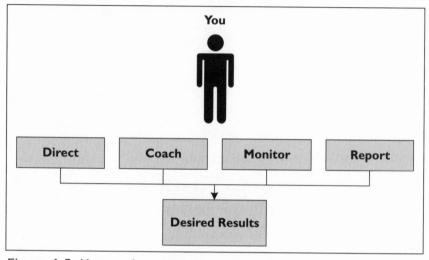

Figure 1-2. You as the manager

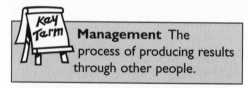 **Management** The process of producing results through other people.

For many managers, this realization requires a shift in mind-set and skills.

A Shift in Mindset and Skills

Think about the job you did before you were promoted to your first management position. What was your primary concern? Unless you were the office gossip, you were most concerned with your job. You concentrated your efforts on what you did.

What was the nature of the work you did? In all likelihood, it was mainly task-oriented. You did work of a technical or operational nature.

But when you occupy a management role, your frame of reference changes. Management requires a different mindset and skills.

The Managerial Mindset

As a manager, your primary focus is no longer on *you*. A manager's mindset shifts to *them* (or, perhaps more appropriately, *us*), the employees who do the tasks. Although you're still concerned with yourself in terms of doing your job well, you recognize your success depends in large part on how well you and your employees work together to accomplish goals. You concentrate on doing the things that will equip and encourage them to produce the desired results—and many of those things you do involve communication.

Management Skill

As a worker, you probably prided yourself on your technical or operational skills. It's likely one of the reasons you were promoted to management. You performed the tasks better than other employees.

Now, you don't do those same tasks anymore. You oversee the performance of others who do them. Your effectiveness as a manager isn't determined by your expertise with tasks or technicalities. Your effectiveness resides in your *relational* skills.

> **Key Term**
>
> **Relational skills** Skills that build and maintain relationships. They pertain to how well you read people and relate to them. Relational skills include the abilities to establish rapport, instill trust, foster cooperation, form alliances, persuade, mediate conflict, and communicate clearly and constructively.

To be effective, you need to be a skillful communicator. You need to be especially skilled at *interpersonal* communications.

The Importance of Interpersonal Communication

Interpersonal skills are increasingly critical because of four factors of growing importance in most organizations these days: technology, time intensity, diversity, and liability.

> **Key Term**
>
> **Interpersonal communication** Person-to-person and (with the exception of telephone and e-mail messages) face-to-face conversation. The prefix *inter* means *among* or *between*, so interpersonal is not one-way communication. It's an exchange that occurs through dialogue between two people or through discussion among several, with participation by everyone involved.

Technology

Review what you do. How much of your workday is spent interacting with people face-to-face compared with interacting with technology? How do you think employees would answer the question?

In an edition of a respected dictionary dated 1987, the word "e-mail" doesn't appear. Now, e-mail is commonplace. So is voice-mail. Every year, the ranks of telecommuters grow. Technology has transformed the workplace, and its influence and impact are growing.

As early as 1982, social forecaster John Naisbitt cautioned in *Megatrends* (1982, p. 39), "Whenever new technology is introduced into society, there must be a counter-balancing human response—that is, *high touch*." When you skillfully interact person-to-person, you bring to an increasingly high-tech workplace the necessary high-touch. (That's a key theme in Chapter 9, "E-Communications.")

Time Intensity

The workplace is hurried. ASAP isn't soon enough. You need it NOW! (Or better yet, yesterday.) Rarely are documents sent by so-called "snail-mail." They're transmitted electronically in nanoseconds or expressed for overnight delivery. Like many other people, you've probably learned the modern method for getting more done in less time: multi-tasking.

You're pressed for time. But Joe has a problem he has to talk to you about. The clock is ticking. But Jane doesn't know the next step to take on that project until she gets further direction from you. In a rush, you "cut to the chase"—get right to the point—no time for idle chitchat. And Paul in human resources perceives you're rude. What about the employee who comes to you with a valid concern? You may miss it if you're multi-tasking because multi-tasking diverts your attention.

When time is at a premium, you can't afford to waste time through incomplete, inaccurate, or ineffective communication. Good interpersonal skills enable you to make the best use of the time you spend interacting with people.

Diversity

What is the population of your organization like? If it's like most, it's diverse. Age, ethnic, and gender diversity are commonplace. In addition to obvious differences, there are less obvious ones, like political preferences, religious beliefs, and lifestyle.

Jane asks for a day off to celebrate Kwanza. Joe is offended by off-color jokes. Paul winces when you greet him with "Hey, dude!" Arturo is free to work late every night. Dave is a single parent who needs to get home to his kids.

And you? To be fully effective, you need to be attuned to the various needs, interests, priorities, and communication styles of employees, peers, and the boss. You need to be adept at drawing upon the respective talents of a diverse work group. To do that, you need to interact—interpersonally. (This is so important that we get into it right away, in the first two chapters, devoted to perceptions, profiles, and preferences.)

Liability

In recent years, organizations have been sued by employees for every conceivable reason. Some legal actions have merit. Others should never go as far as they do. Many issues could be resolved when they first surface at the departmental level—if the manager knows what's going on and steps up to it.

You need to "keep your ear to the ground," so to speak. You want to build with employees relationships that encourage them to first bring their concerns to you. When employees have a grievance, take the time and show a willingness to hear them out. Use your interpersonal skills to help resolve issues before they get out of hand.

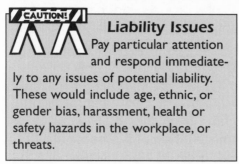

Handle with Care

Never appear to take lightly what someone else takes seriously. You may think a concern an employee expresses is "no big deal." But if it's important to him or her, respond as though it's important to you. If you don't, it'll become important to you when you have to deal with the backlash that may occur.

If you laugh off or make light of a matter someone considers serious, you risk offending that person. They'll feel you don't take *them* seriously.

You can minimize the likelihood of unwarranted legal action. How? Foster an atmosphere of open communication. Without it, employees conclude their ideas don't matter and their concerns are of no concern to you. They may think an issue management should address is being ignored. Resentments brew.

Address interpersonal conflicts early on. If you don't, one of two things will happen. The conflict will escalate or it'll be repressed. If it's repressed, it will recur. You can bet on it.

Unresolved concerns and ongoing conflicts foment an environment rife with resentments and hostilities. As a result, it's

Liability Issues

Pay particular attention and respond immediately to any issues of potential liability. These would include age, ethnic, or gender bias, harassment, health or safety hazards in the workplace, or threats.

ripe for litigation. A discontented and disgruntled employee will sometimes look for an excuse to sue.

The combined effects of these four factors— technology, time intensity, diversity, and liability— make strong interpersonal skills a "must." So do the characteristics of contemporary organizations.

Interactions in a Contemporary Organization

You can see at a glance some of the obvious differences between contemporary and old-order organizations, two extremes on the management continuum.

A contemporary organization is flatter. Within it, interactions are more fluid. And it places a premium on feedback. More people report to any one manager, and there are fewer managers. Teams are common,

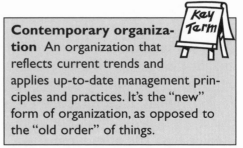

Contemporary organization An organization that reflects current trends and applies up-to-date management principles and practices. It's the "new" form of organization, as opposed to the "old order" of things.

and communication networks allow people to interact with each other quickly and easily. Let's look at some of the characteristics of the contemporary organization in more detail.

Flattened

In recent years, many organizations have dismantled the old hierarchical form. The multiple levels of a traditional structure have been reduced and replaced with self-managed teams or cross-functional work groups. The "chain of command" is neither as long nor as rigid. Some of the traditional formalities have dissolved, allowing interactions to occur on a more casual basis.

As a former manager in a highly hierarchical corporation, I can remember when you wouldn't think of addressing the CEO in any way other than "Mr. Karey" ("Sir" was implied by a deferential tone of voice). Now, it's not uncommon in some companies to wave at the CEO from across the room and, with a tone of good-friend familiarity, shout out, "Hi, Joan!"

Know the Norms Even in the most contemporary organizations, there's still such a thing as "corporate etiquette." There are protocols and courtesies all employees are expected to observe. Many organizations, for example, still frown on going over the boss's head. If you go over the boss's head, you do so at your own risk. Know the "unwritten rules" and norms of acceptable conduct where you work. And let your employees know what they are, too, so they don't inadvertently cross the line and commit a breach of etiquette.

Fluid

An old-order organization is like a skyscraper. Navigating through its many levels can be time-consuming and tedious, especially when you try to elevate an issue from the ground floor to the top.

In contrast, a contemporary organization is like a modern two-story building. You can move between sections with greater ease and speed. Since you don't have to wend your way though and wait for layers of approval, you can respond to situations more rapidly. Often, you have greater access to those "in the know."

You can interact more readily, not only within your own team or department, but across functional lines as well. A contemporary organization allows and even encourages the flow of informal communication between and among interdependent groups.

Because a contemporary form is more "open," you have more avenues for advancing your ideas and the ideas of employees on your team. You also gain greater visibility for yourself and for promotable personnel. Occasions that give you visibility, such as meetings and presentations with executives, are opportunities to showcase your relational skills. (We'll cover meetings in Chapter 7 and presentations in Chapter 8.)

Feedback

In an old-order organization, communication is often one-way. A manager "above" communicates "down" to employees. In a contemporary organization, the manager resides at the center of the team or work group and everyone works within the context of delivering products and services to customers.

Your communications radiate out to employees. They, in turn, convey their feedback to you (and to one another). And there is regular communication with customers as well.

Contemporary organizations strive to be "people-sensitive"—responsive to the needs of employees and customers. Interactions are dynamic. There's more give-and-take, with ideas and information freely exchanged.

Employees don't have to hunt high and low for a suggestion box. They know managers are receptive to hearing their

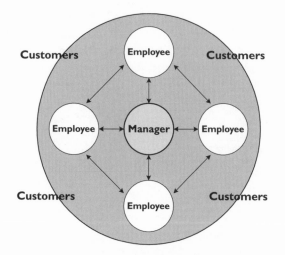

Figure 1-3. The contemporary approach to managing

suggestions firsthand. Asked for their input, employees feel valued. Managers find it easier to achieve "buy-in" because employees have had a say in decisions they're asked to support.

In any type of organization, old or new or something in between, you get better results when you interact with people on a regular basis. When you do, keep your communications constructive.

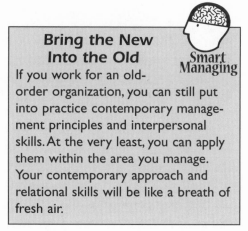

Bring the New Into the Old

If you work for an old-order organization, you can still put into practice contemporary management principles and interpersonal skills. At the very least, you can apply them within the area you manage. Your contemporary approach and relational skills will be like a breath of fresh air.

The ABCs of Constructive Communication

As the term implies, *constructive* communication builds up. It builds up employee morale. It builds teamwork. It builds positive relationships between people who then are not only willing, but eager to work in concert.

> **⚠ CAUTION!**
>
> ## Out with the Old
>
> Beware *the John Wayne style of management,* an approach often used in old-order organizations. It takes its name from those post-World War II movies in which John Wayne played the role of conquering hero.
>
> Picture John Wayne standing on the bow of a battleship. He spots the enemy approaching. He commands the troops, "Fire!" What do they do? They obey.
>
> Now picture John Wayne managing your department. He sees the need for action. He shouts a command. "Fire!" What do employees do? Nowadays, they might ask "Why?" "What's in it for me?" "Do I get overtime pay?"
>
> Shouting orders and expecting blind obedience is outdated and ineffective. Although military metaphors are still prevalent in business circles, managers act less and less like John Wayne commanding the troops. As a rule, you'll get better results when you elicit cooperation rather than demand compliance. Remember, if you don't like commands made of you, why would you do that to others?
>
> One exception to the rule is in emergency or crisis situations. Then, the situation calls for a John Wayne type to take charge. The troops recognize the need to follow the leader's directions. Brainstorming and decision-making by consensus are postponed until the crisis is over.

Destructive communication triggers conflict. It breeds dissension and divisiveness. It results in resistance and, on occasion, outright rebellion. It creates enemies rather than allies.

Booker T. Washington observed, "There are two ways of exerting one's strength: one is pushing down, the other is pulling up." The point sums up the contrast between destructive and constructive communication.

Whenever you interact with people—whether employees, colleagues, or the boss—you have essentially the same two ways to exert your influence. You can "push down" by putting people down. Or you can "pull up" by communicating constructively.

In the physical sense of exerting strength, pushing down is easier than pulling up. In the relational sense of exerting influence, putting down is also easier. Harsh criticism, sniping remarks, and cutting people off are examples of communication that puts down.

It doesn't take skill to put people down. Anyone can do it. But the price is high, especially for a manager. Putting down demeans people, who are then disinclined to give you their best performance or support. They may be inclined to sabotage your efforts instead.

Pulling up through constructive communication takes skill. Sometimes it takes more time. But it reaps noticeably better responses and results. In the long run, it makes your job easier and interactions more pleasant. And you gain the added advantage of being seen as someone who can bring out the best in people. That's an asset if you want to advance in your career.

Throughout this book, you'll find skills and techniques for dealing constructively with specific situations. The ABCs described next apply *every* time you interact with someone. They are the fundamental principles of constructive communication. They form the foundation upon which productive relationships are built.

Approach

If you've flown in an airplane, you know the approach is critical to making a smooth landing. If a pilot attempted to land a plane without giving thought to the approach, trouble would certainly follow.

Have you ever experienced a troublesome interaction with an employee? with your boss? Part of the problem may have been with your approach. Communications proceed more smoothly and constructively when your approach is positive.

> **Key Term**
>
> **Approach** The manner of addressing both a person and the subject. It's the preface to a communication, something that sets the stage. From a speaker's approach, a listener forms expectations of what's coming next.

To approach a person in a positive manner, be pleasant and gracious. When appropriate, smile sincerely. A smile ranks high among likability factors and helps to put people at ease.

> **Key Term**
>
> **Confidence** An attribute of a positive approach and a trademark of skillful communicators. Confidence is synonymous with self-assurance. Confidence shores you up to remain calm and composed, even under pressure. When you convey confidence, people are more inclined to place their confidence in you.
>
> Confidence is not arrogance. Arrogance is unwarranted conceit. It's evidence of an enlarged ego. When people are approached arrogantly, most react negatively.

If the subject isn't pleasant, such as when you're the bearer of bad news, consider the most positive quality you can project to the person under the circumstances. Some situations call for empathy or an expression of genuine concern. Other times, it's best to adopt a matter-of-fact manner.

To approach the subject in a positive manner, be well prepared. Know what you're going to say. Early on in your message, allude to some benefit the listener stands to gain by hearing you out.

It's always positive when you approach a person respectfully, treat the subject reasonably, and convey confidence. Keep this in mind as you read this book: every technique works better with the right approach.

In later chapters, you'll find out more about positive approaches to specific situations and positive attributes to add to your communications. For now, store in your memory bank this "A" of the fundamental ABCs: *approach* in a positive manner to set the stage for a pleasant and productive interaction.

Build Bridges

Imagine you're about to undertake a project of building a bridge across a river. You're going to do this in partnership with someone you interact with frequently. It may be an employee, a peer, or your boss.

Picture yourself standing on one side of the river. They're standing on the opposite bank. It's been determined that the best way to build this bridge is if each of you works from your respective sides toward the center. The bridge will be complete when the halves are joined in the middle.

Refrain from Labeling

Labeling is a form of typecasting. A label is a "what" that can interfere with seeing "who" a person truly is. Labeling affects how you think about a person, which affects how you approach them and the communication that follows.

Suppose, for example, you've labeled Terry a "troublemaker." When you approach Terry, what's running through your mind? "Ugh, I've got to talk to the troublemaker." Negative thinking like that is sure to show in your approach to Terry and throughout your interaction. How do you communicate with a "troublemaker"? Guardedly or aggressively. How will Terry react? Very likely like the "troublemaker" you've labeled Terry to be.

People tend to live up—or down—to your expectations. Critical, disparaging labels convey negative expectations and evoke behaviors on your part that quite naturally trigger negative reactions from others. If you must label people, give them positive labels, like Terry "the trooper." And think it with a smile.

Now translate this hypothetical situation into what goes on when people interact. In conversations, discussions, meetings, or presentations, see yourself as being engaged in bridge building. The bridge you're building is called *productive working relationship*.

That's the aim of interpersonal communications: to build a relationship. Your ultimate goal is to have securely in place a relationship from which both people derive benefit. In a productive relationship between a manager and employee, the manager gains the benefits of the employee's best efforts and input, such as creative ideas and suggestions for solving problems. The employee receives the benefits of the manager's guidance, feedback that helps the employee improve their skills and performance, support for

Respect The quality of showing consideration and taking care to deal with people thoughtfully.

Respect does not require that you like someone personally. It doesn't mean you have to agree with or even always understand them. It does require viewing a person as a fellow human being who has intrinsic value.

Understanding and Cooperation

Smart Managing Do you and most of the people with whom you interact often understand and cooperate with one another? Or do you find that a lack of understanding and poor cooperation creates obstacles to performance and productivity?

As you progress through this book, pay particular attention to the interpersonal skills that will help you foster understanding and cooperation. By training and coaching, help your employees develop those skills so that they, too, can apply them in their interactions with you and with each other.

good ideas, motivation, and perhaps mentoring. Both receive from one another the benefit of being treated with respect.

Like building a bridge, building a relationship takes time, attention, and skill. It also often entails bridging differences. And sometimes you have to meet people halfway.

The middle of our metaphorical bridge represents points at which you and your bridge-building partner understand one another. It's when you say, "I see what you're getting at," and you really do. And if you don't understand, you try harder. Understanding one another, you're more willing to cooperate with one another.

When, for example, you understand employees' goals, you can cooperate with them to help them attain their goals. When they understand your concern about a problem, they can cooperate with you to get it solved.

Bridges hold up only if they're constructed on a firm foundation. The same is true of relationships. A cooperative, productive working relationship is based on a twofold foundation of trust and commonality.

Key Term **Trust** The firm belief that someone or something is reliable, that you can depend on them or it.

Trust is included as a key term because it's key to how effective you will be in your dealings with people. It's a vital component of constructive communications.

Trust

To trust, people must feel safe. They need to feel safe not only in the sense of their physical safety and security, but in emotional and psychological ways as well.

Trust in organizations has eroded. The lack of trust can be attributed in part to more than a decade of downsizings and lay-offs. Many employees feel they can no longer trust that they'll have a job from one year to the next. Lack of trust can be attributed in part to the experience of frequent change, which is often accompanied by uncertainty and insecurity.

For these reasons, it's important that you interact in trustworthy ways. Employees may not trust the organization, but you want them to trust *you*.

When people feel they can trust you, they're inclined to be honest with you in turn. They're more willing to give you their support. When you need employees to perform "above and beyond the call of duty," most will come through for you—if they trust you.

You develop trust when you show yourself to be trustworthy. Through your communication behaviors, you convey the unspoken message, "You're safe with me."

When you interact with people, preserve their self-esteem. Refrain from making potentially hurtful or demeaning remarks about anybody. Most people feel uneasy hearing such remarks, even if they aren't directed at them. They suspect the next remark might be. Such remarks also come across as personal attacks that put a person on guard. When someone feels the need to be guarded or defensive, it's a clear sign they don't trust.

When someone shares a confidence with you, keep it confidential. If they learn you disclosed their secret, they won't feel they can safely open up to you.

Take care that you don't punish people with the past. If an employee makes a mistake, confront the matter and get it corrected. Once you're satisfied the employee is on the right track concerning that matter, move on.

If they make a mistake a year later, don't harp on the "sins" of the past. Don't say things like "A year ago you goofed on the Jones account. Now you've made a mistake on the Smith project." Here's how the employee translates that statement in their mind: "What's wrong with you? Don't you ever learn?" If you

Consistency Creates Trust

Smart Managing   People come to trust what they can count on, what occurs consistently.

Try this exercise. Across the top of a sheet of paper, write: "I can be counted on to ..." List things you do consistently. Be honest! For example:

"... do what I say I'm going to do."

"... reprimand employees in front of their peers."

"... listen without interrupting."

"... tell people what I think they want to hear rather than the straight scoop."

"... go to bat for the people I manage."

"... take credit for other people's ideas."

Now, which of those consistent behaviors build trust? Which undermine trust?

What next? Borrow a line from an old song: "Accentuate the positive, eliminate the negative." Continue consistently doing the trust builders (and add to them). Work on improving any behaviors that undermine trust.

You might also find it useful to introduce this exercise to the employees you manage. If you do, be sure to present it with a positive approach.

punish a person with the past, they won't feel safe interacting with you now or in the future.

Commonality

It's a characteristic of human nature. We prefer dealing with people who are "like" us. It's easier to understand one another when we share some things in common: a common language, similar backgrounds, common interests. We'll cooperate more readily with those with whom we have things in common.

Considering the many differences that exist in diverse work groups, one of your challenges is to discover and develop commonalities.

Commonality unites people. Drawn together by what they share, people function more effectively as a team. Commonalities reduce conflict. When conflict does occur, a step to resolving it is to identify the interests and goals in common.

A method for bridging differences and building commonalities is to engage people in participative planning (the operative word being *participative*). Schedule several sessions over a period of time. You can lead the discussion yourself, bring in a professional facilitator, or delegate discussion leadership to a respected member of your staff who's a skillful communicator.

As you proceed, elicit input from everyone. Encourage exchange. Take care that no one monopolizes the discussion. The point is to get everyone involved and talking about what matters to them.

Start with a discussion of organizational and individual values. What do people believe is the right and ethical way for themselves and the organization to operate? Then develop a mission statement. What is the purpose of the organization? What group of customers does it serve and how will it maximize its ability to serve them? If your organization already has a mission statement, you might ask employees to translate it into one that applies specifically to the operations of your work group. Continue with a discussion that leads to agreement on the group's goals.

These discussions are intended to focus on finding things all of you in the work group have in common. In the future, when differences threaten to disrupt teamwork or productivity, you can redirect the group's attention to their shared values, mission, and goals.

Consider, creatively, activities you can schedule

A Case of Commonality

We'd worked in the same department for over a year. Our desks were adjacent to one another. Since our jobs took us out of the office frequently, we didn't have much occasion to interact during the day. The times we were both in the office, our conversations were brief. On the surface, it appeared we had little in common.

When the company scheduled a weekend "working retreat" for a planning session, we were assigned to be roommates. We arrived on a Friday night. By the time we left on Sunday afternoon, we'd discovered we had a lot in common. From then on, our working relationship was a model of mutual respect and collaboration.

or sponsor that will give employees opportunities to get to know one another—not as coworkers but as individuals. Ask for their ideas. Talk to colleagues to learn about things they've done. With your peers or boss, brainstorm ideas for bringing people together in situations through which they can discover their commonalities.

Customize Your Communication

Joe quickly gets to the "bottom line." He thinks "small talk" is for small minds. He grows impatient in meetings. He cuts people off when they take too long to get to the point.

Paul is a friendly fellow. He pauses to make "small talk," which he considers a way to build rapport with his coworkers and the boss. He listens intently in meetings, often asking questions so he has the complete picture. When relating information, he provides ample detail to make sure he's presenting his points clearly and accurately.

Two different employees with very different modes of communicating. What's yours? Are you more like Joe? More like Paul? Or maybe somewhere in between? How would you describe your manner of interacting with people? Here's the skilled communicator's answer: "I'm flexible."

From the moment you (a) approach a person, and then (b) build a bridge of a productive relationship, you'll experience greater success when you (c) customize your communications to suit the other person.

To customize something means making it specially for a customer. Think of the people you interact with as "customers" who do business with you. Your goal is to provide the highest level of customer satisfaction. When it comes to interpersonal communications, you customize by adapting your mode of communicating to the mode the customer prefers, the mode that works best.

Customizing your communication helps to build trust. It conveys a sense of commonality. But it's not manipulative. It should just demonstrate a sensitivity to different styles of communication and personalities, such that communication is as open as

---

The Real Thing

Have you ever had an experience similar to this one? Two colleagues attend a seminar. In a conversation with them a day or so later, they use a phrase you've never heard them use before. They do something that strikes you as phony. You call them on it. "Where'd that come from?" "Oh," one of them answers, "I picked it up at that seminar."

Call to mind a person you consider an excellent communicator—and a model manager. What are some of the qualities they convey? Sincerity is probably one. A person I consider an outstanding communicator and an exceptional leader is often described as "the genuine article."

Learning new skills and techniques is commendable. It's a way to improve your performance, build better relationships, and advance in your career. But, in the process of trying new techniques, you don't want people thinking the techniques are "tricks." You don't want to come across as contrived, manipulative, or phony.

So practice the skills you learn here. Periodically review the chapters in this book you find most useful for you. Get together with a friend or colleague and role-play. Practice to the point of integrating the skills so they come easily and naturally to you.

---

possible to facilitate your mutual success. This style tends to make people more receptive to what you have to say. And, in most cases, it prompts from them a more favorable response.

How do you customize your communications? You'll find out in Chapter 3.

The Communicator's Checklist for Chapter 1

❑ Because communication is critical to what you do, it pays to hone your skills.

❑ In view of the nature of the workplace today, interpersonal skills are more important than ever before.

❑ Apply the ABCs of constructive communication whenever you interact with people. Approach in a positive manner. Build bridges of understanding and cooperation, based on trust and commonalities. Customize your communications to suit others.

The Part Perceptions Play

Previously, you'd stopped by the break room for coffee. A few employees seated around a table in the corner abruptly stopped talking when you entered the room. Over the next few days, you get the impression people are avoiding you. During a staff meeting, a couple of employees snicker. You wonder—no, you worry about what's going on. Leaving work on Friday, you resolve to find out first thing next week.

When you arrive at work Monday morning, the employees are gathered in the lobby. They greet you with a shout of "SUR-PRISE! Happy Birthday!" The break room is decorated with streamers and balloons. You're aghast. "Are you *really* surprised?" the receptionist asks. Are you ever! Judging from the behavior you'd observed the previous week, you'd perceived something was amiss. The incident reminds you: impressions can be misleading.

The Power of Perceptions

Have you ever found yourself in situations like these? You send an e-mail to all employees. One or two are angered by what you wrote. Walking by an employee's desk, you make a friendly comment meant in jest. Later, you learn the employee was upset by your remark. At a staff meeting, you present a new policy. During the

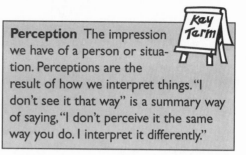

Perception The impression we have of a person or situation. Perceptions are the result of how we interpret things. "I don't see it that way" is a summary way of saying, "I don't perceive it the same way you do. I interpret it differently."

discussion that follows, it's evident several employees misinterpret the intent of the policy.

You shake your head, wondering why they didn't "get it."

You try to correct a misunderstanding by explaining, "That's not what I meant." You realize that communicating effectively involves more than merely putting words together. You need to consider how your message will be perceived.

Message A generic term that refers to any communication, spoken or written, long or short. A comment made in passing, a two-line e-mail, a two-hour formal presentation, a 200-page report—all are messages.

How Perceptions Take Shape

Communication training commonly refers to two roles: sender and receiver. It's more accurate to describe the roles as sender and *perceiver*. It's also more useful because it calls to mind the principal part perceptions play in every communication exchange.

When you communicate, whether in spoken or written form, here's what happens:

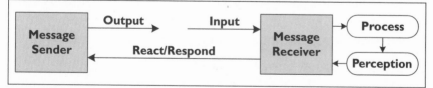

Figure 2-1. The communication process

The message you send is your output. To the person who receives it, it's their input. When we receive input, we process it and form perceptions. In short:

Perception = Reception + Processing

A communication is processed through an individual's frame of reference. Our frame of reference is made up of a multitude of factors:

- Attitude
- Beliefs
- Cultural conventions
- Education
- Emotional state at the time
- Experience
- Gender

Naturally, one person's frame of reference differs from another's. Consider a situation as simple as your saying, "Good morning" when you arrive at work. One employee smiles and cheerfully responds, "Good morning." Another glares and snipes back, "Yeah, what's so good about it?!" And the boss, who's at work at the crack of dawn every day, remarks, "You're late." Same message sent. Same message received. But different frames of reference produce different perceptions, which in turn generate different replies.

The processing that shapes perceptions occurs with lightning speed and usually subconsciously. Much of the time, our minds form impressions, make judgments, and come to conclusions without our consciously thinking about it. It happens automatically.

Be aware that, whenever you communicate, perceptions are taking shape. And they have a significant impact on interactions, because perceptions condition how people respond or react.

Perception Is More Powerful than Fact

We respond to messages based on what we *perceive* to be true, more so than on what may be true in fact. Even if the facts differ from a person's perception of what's going on, perception

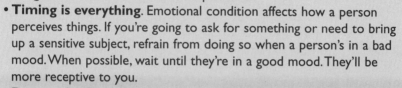

> ## Tap into Their Frame of Reference
> **Smart Managing**
> The better you understand another person's frame of refer-
> ence, the more effective your communications with them will
> be. In general, bear in mind these helpful hints.
> - **Timing is everything**. Emotional condition affects how a person
>   perceives things. If you're going to ask for something or need to bring
>   up a sensitive subject, refrain from doing so when a person's in a bad
>   mood. When possible, wait until they're in a good mood. They'll be
>   more receptive to you.
> - **Perspective**. Typically, managers and employees have different per-
>   spectives—another factor that affects perceptions. Employees some-
>   times form inaccurate perceptions of a manager, or of what a manager
>   directs them to do, simply because they don't have the benefit of the
>   "bigger picture" like you do. Either present points to employees from
>   *their* perspective or provide information that acquaints them with the
>   broader view.
> - **Cultural Factors**. If you work in a culturally diverse workplace, be
>   sensitive to cultural differences. Do you manage employees for whom
>   English is a second language? If so, recognize their vocabulary may be
>   more limited than yours. Refrain from using idiomatic expressions that
>   may lead to misperceptions. Be aware of mannerisms that may be
>   offensive to people whose cultural conventions differ from yours. And if
>   you do business internationally, you'll find it's beneficial to expand your
>   skills through specialized training in cross-cultural communications.

wins out. Perceptions, in other words, exert a powerful influence on behavior because they represent our interpretation of the facts. And that's what we respond to—our impressions of people and our interpretations of events.

Suppose, for example, that the company you work for announces a merger with a corporation that's the leader in your industry. Assume that the merger is, in fact, good for your company. Employees who perceive the positive potential of the merger will respond affirmatively. But if some perceive it's bad news, prepare for a negative reaction.

In his book, *The Pursuit of WOW!* management consultant and best-selling author Tom Peters points out, "Perception is all there is—manage it!" The point is especially pertinent to managers. You may recall from Chapter 1 that management is about producing results through the performance of others. People are much more inclined to give you their best performance when they have positive perceptions of you and of what you're striving to do.

You have two sets of perceptions to manage: yours and theirs. Let's consider first how to manage other people's perceptions.

Often, you don't know, and certainly don't control, what goes on in another person's mind. You can't manage how someone processes the inputs they receive. But you can manage the outputs you send. How? By the *cues* you convey when you communicate.

Communication Cues

Communication occurs through three types of cues:

- **Verbal**—the words and phrases you use
- **Vocal**—the characteristics of your voice when you speak
- **Visual**—everything the perceiver sees

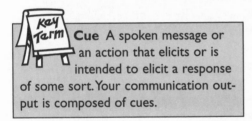

Cue A spoken message or an action that elicits or is intended to elicit a response of some sort. Your communication output is composed of cues.

The relative impact of each type varies, depending on the mode of communication. When you interact with people face to face, visual and vocal cues almost always have a greater impact than the words you use. In telephone conversations, without evident visual cues, the vocal and verbal are prominent. In written communications (including e-mail), word choice and the the level of formality they suggest are crucial. In every mode of communication, cues color the perceptions that form in the mind of your listener or reader. Ideally, all of the cues you convey will combine to create a favorable impression.

Verbal Cues

In face-to-face communication, usually the actual words you say make less of an impression than how you sound and how you look when you say them. Notice I said "usually." By a well-considered choice of words, you can increase the positive impact of your verbal cues. That includes not using words that have negative implications, no matter how you express them—like "hot-button" words.

Hot-Button Words

These words push people's buttons. They usually instigate unfavorable perceptions and subsequently trigger negative reactions. Often, they're associated with aggressive or insensitive communicators or with people who lack professionalism. In fact, that may not be the case (but remember, perception is more powerful than fact). Sometimes, we use such words simply because we're "parroting." We've heard them repeatedly and parrot or mimic what we've heard.

The bad news is many of us use words without thinking about the effect they have. The good news is communication is learned. When we're aware of words that generate negative perceptions, we can learn to eliminate such verbal cues from our communications. In general, hot button words and phrases make people become *defensive*. And when someone becomes defensive, it always undermines the cooperation needed to get a job done efficiently and effectively.

There are five types of hot-button words. As you read through the explanations that follow, consider this question. If someone said that to me, what would I perceive?

1. Demanding Words. Hypothetically speaking, suppose your boss said to you, *You have to... You must... I insist... You'd better...* (implying *or else.*). What do you perceive? If you're like many people, you perceive this hypothetical boss is hard-nosed, dictatorial, maybe even threatening.

Here's a common reaction to demanding words. The employee thinks, "Don't tell me what I *have* to do." If they feel their job depends on doing what the manager demands, they'll do it. But they'll do it with resentment. They won't give it their best effort. If a demanding manner is a manager's norm—it's the rule rather than the exception—some employees may even look for ways to sabotage tasks or projects.

People want some sense of control. Employees are empowered, in part, by having choices. Demanding words leave people feeling they have no choice.

You foster favorable perceptions and responses by speaking to people in terms that convey they have options. Use phrasing that suggests there are alternatives, various avenues, different approaches. And convey they have some say in the matter of which to choose.

Instead of saying, "You have to finish this by 3:00," say something like "I need this by 3:00 today. How soon can you get to it?" In the best of all possible worlds, the employee would answer, "Right away. I'll have it for you by 11:00." In reality, the dialogue would sound more like this:

They reply: "No way. I can't possibly do it by then."
You ask: "How long do you think it'll take?"
They say: "A couple of hours, but I have all of these other things to do first."
You say: "This is a top priority. Let's take a look at what you can delegate or defer for now in order to free up your morning to work on this. What do you think?"

Engage employees in dialogue that welcomes their input and offers them options. When you do, you encourage them to be willing to work with you rather than resist and resent dictatorial demands.

2. Demeaning Words. You're in a meeting. The group is discussing a problem with a project. You offer a suggestion about how you think it can be solved. The executive leading the meeting remarks, "That's a *stupid* idea." What do you perceive?

Demeaning words include *stupid, dummy, jerk, nerd*, and *bimbo*, to name a few. They're verbal put-downs that belittle a person. You can say them with a smile and a pleasant tone of voice, but the words themselves break through those vocal and visual cues and hit people where it hurts.

Refrain from saying things like "How could you be so stupid?" or "That was a dumb thing to do." Even if said in jest, words that demean also discourage and demotivate. For a manager, that's the real drawback to demeaning words. If you're going to successfully produce results through the performance of others, you need people who are encouraged and motivated, not discouraged and disgruntled because they've been demeaned.

Remove from your vocabulary the words *fail, failed,* and *failure.* Nothing is more demeaning than to be thought of or, worse, called a failure. A statement like "You failed to make your objectives" can be perceived to mean "I failed, therefore I'm a failure." Instead, phrase it this way: "You neglected to make your objectives" or "The results fell short of objectives."

3. Discriminatory Language. One of your colleagues, Will B. Anonymous, has a vacancy to fill in his department. He asks around, "Does anyone know someone they'd recommend for the job?" He says he's interested only in candidates of a certain gender and age who have an MBA from the Ivy League university he graduated from. What if you don't match any of his criteria? What do you perceive?

Discriminatory words convey partiality or prejudice. Managers who use discriminatory language run the risk of being perceived as unfair. Worse, voicing outright bias can be a violation of the antidiscrimination laws. On this point, the old adage applies, "Better safe than sorry." Refrain from making inappropriate or possibly hurtful references to age, gender, sexual orientation, race, ethnicity, religion, political affiliation, disabilities, or characteristics of a purely personal nature. You want to be seen as someone who makes personnel decisions on the basis of job performance, not personal prejudices.

4. Potentially Offensive Language. Coming back from lunch, you walk through the department adjacent to yours. You overhear the manager of that department conversing with an employee. The manager's language is peppered with expletives: #%!# this and #%!# that. What do you perceive?

In a society in which it sometimes seems "Anything goes," you may perceive "No big deal." But from a manager especially, profanity is a big deal. It's inappropriate in the workplace. It conveys a lack of professionalism. And using profane language or telling off-color jokes displays a lack of regard for those who may be offended by obscenities.

As a manager, you can't afford the luxury of blurting out whatever comes to mind because you can't afford the risk of giving offense. What you say in the privacy of your own home or in social situations is, of course, your business. But what you say in the workplace—in the presence of your boss, colleagues, and employees—is the business of the business.

If you use profanity at work, it gives employees an excuse to use profanity, which can have unfortunate consequences. If executives visit your department and hear employees using foul language as a habit, what will they perceive? Do you work in an area that deals with customers or the public, in person or over the phone? If they hear obscenities they find offensive, what will they perceive?

5. No and Can't. In a conversation with your boss, you mention you want to advance in your career. Your boss says, "I can't put you on the promotable list. You don't have the qualifications." What do you perceive?

Suppose your boss said instead, "As soon as you complete the training for certification, I'll be glad to consider you for promotion." How does that change your perception?

Negative words like "No" and "can't" stir up negative feelings. The employee who hears "can't" from a manager may perceive "It's not that you *can't*. What you really mean is you *won't*." Now they don't feel good about you because they've formed the impression that (a) you're not willing to consider what they've asked and (b) you weren't up-front with them about it. They don't feel good about themselves because "can't" causes them to question, "What's wrong with me that I can't be promoted?"

If you're tempted to use negative words, rephrase what you're going to say in a positive way. For example, instead of saying,

"No, that's not possible," tell people what is possible. Rather than relating what can't be done, communicate what can be.

An added advantage to your speaking in "Yes, can do" terms is that you set an example for others to follow. You may recall from a previous example the employee who said, "No way. I can't possibly do it by then." Imagine how much easier and more pleasant your job would be if every employee were taking positive cues from you and saying, "Let me see what I *can* do."

You're aware of the hot-button words that typically trigger negative perceptions and reactions. As you manage your output in terms of the verbal cues you communicate, it's also useful to be aware of worn-out words.

Worn-Out Words

Words get worn out by overuse. Because they've been used so often and in so many contexts, they make little or no impres-

---

Better than "But"

When used as a conjunction, the word "but" puts people on guard. It has the effect of negating the point in the clause that precedes it. What do you perceive when you hear or read the following?

"I like your idea, but ...."

"You've done a good job, but ..."

Realizing the negative effect of "but," some people have taken to using "however" instead. Listeners and readers have grown wise to this trick. "However" now has the same negative effect as "but." To avoid using "but," simply end the sentence or use the word "and" in its place:

"I like your idea. I feel it's only fair to tell you we don't have the budget to fund it."

"You've done a good job. And I have a suggestion for how you can do even better."

"Here's what I like about your idea. I also have some concerns. Let's see if we can deal with them in a constructive manner."

The one time "but" has a positive effect is when it's followed by good news. For example, "As you know, the budget is tight this year, but you'll still be getting a year-end bonus."

TRICKS OF THE TRADE

sion. In some cases, worn-out words have vague or various meanings and can be easily misconstrued. So use them sparingly or not at all.

Worn-out words fall into one of two categories.

1. Hackneyed Phrases. Over the course of your career, how many conferences and meetings have you attended? How many times have you heard the phrase "challenges and opportunities"? What do you perceive it to mean? When you hear it, what response does it elicit?

Common reactions to that expression range from an indifferent "Ho-hum, here we go again" to a frantic "Oh, no, we've got big problems!" The bridge of communication breaks down.

When people hear stale phrases, some stop listening. They perceive they're about to be told what they've heard many times before. Others listen but misinterpret the message because the communication isn't clear and complete.

How many times have you heard these well-worn phrases? "Teamwork is the name of the game." "Work smarter, not harder." "When the going gets tough, the tough get going."

If you're inclined to use a hackneyed phrase, first ask yourself these questions. What does that mean? Hearing or reading this, what will people perceive? What point do I really want to get across? Then come up with a fresh way to express what you have to say.

2. Buzz Words. These are the acronyms, abbreviations, and catch words best known as business jargon. Among like-minded people, they function as a kind of verbal shorthand. In recent years, business jargon has been inundated with buzz words like "leading edge," "TQM," "paradigm," "strategies," "globalization," "24/7," and "e-" (as in "e-mail," "e-trade," "e-commerce," and, in a televised commercial with a humorous twist, "e-nough").

Although buzz words are a staple of business communications, there are drawbacks to using them repeatedly. Over time, they grow stale and people tire of hearing them. The impact they initially had is diluted through overuse. If you're communicating with someone who's unfamiliar with the buzz words you use, your message will lack meaning. If their understanding of the buzz word differs from yours, your message may be misinterpreted. This doesn't mean you don't use terms like e-mail, for example. But it does mean use them judiciously when they will then have real meaning to listeners.

Verbal Cues to Use

A precept of good customer service is "Make it easy and pleasant for customers to do business with you." A similar precept applies to good communication. Make it easy and pleasant for people to interact with you. You do that, in part, by applying the following "rules" for verbal cues.

1. Straight Talk. Make your message plain. Don't confuse your communications with gobbledygook or unnecessary verbiage. Minimize the likelihood of being misinterpreted. Use words your listener or reader will clearly understand.

Be careful that you don't come across as being blunt. But do get to the heart of the matter in a straightforward manner. Don't mince words or talk around a topic as though you're trying to avoid the subject. People prefer to be dealt with honestly and directly. That's the impression you want to give.

2. Specifics. The chart below lists commonly used words. The first two are shown as examples. On the blank line next to each word, write a number between 0 and 100 that indicates the meaning in terms of the amount of something the word implies.

0	Nothing/Never
100	Everything/Always
_____	Many
_____	Few
_____	Most
_____	Some
_____	Often
_____	Seldom
_____	Substantial amount
_____	Minimal increase

Ask each of the employees you manage to complete this exercise. Compare your answers with theirs.

What do these words mean? You'll discover they mean whatever each person perceives them to mean.

When you want to make sure people accurately interpret your meaning, be specific.

On some occasions, being specific doesn't matter much. In a casual conversation with a friend, you agree you'll "do lunch soon." What does that mean? It could mean you'll meet for lunch next week or never. Either way, there aren't serious consequences to being vague in such a situation.

Other times, being specific matters a great deal. Suppose you're presenting a mid-year report to the executive board. You say, "My department has shown a substantial increase in productivity." By *substantial*, you mean a 10% increase. Members of the board perceive *substantial* to mean that you doubled productivity. Imagine how disappointed they'll be when, upon reading the written report, they discover you "lied."

Of course, you didn't lie. You neglected to specify. But when there's a disparity between what a person perceives to be true and what is true in fact, which usually carries the greater weight? Perception. Their perception is their truth. And anything else is seen as a lie.

⚠ CAUTION!

ASAP

What does it mean? As Soon As Possible. And what does *that* mean? To you, it's an abbreviated way of saying, "This is urgent. I need it *now*." But the person receiving an ASAP message may think, "It's not possible for me to get to this now. Next week will be soon enough." Or they conveniently take it to mean At Some Advanced Point in time.

Don't use "ASAP" unless you're willing to wait or unless you specify what you mean by "soon."

---

3. Courtesies. When it comes to managing perceptions, you want to give thought not only to how people perceive *your message*, but also to how they perceive *you*. You'll promote more positive perceptions of you when you communicate courteously. Make a habit of saying those simple but significant words that convey courtesy: *please, thank you, you're welcome, may I?* and *excuse me.* Say them with a smile and sincerity.

Notice the difference it makes. Two employees are in a deep discussion about a project they're working on jointly. You break in and interrupt. What do they perceive about you? You're rude.

Or you wait for a break in their conversation and politely say, "Excuse me. May I interrupt for a moment?" You pause to wait for an answer. In this instance, what do they perceive? You're courteous and considerate of them. Which perception will foster more favorable working relationships? Clearly, the latter.

4. I to You. You delegated an important task to an employee. They completed it ahead of schedule and exceeded your expectations. You're going to thank them, in person or with a handwritten note.

You could say, "I'm pleased with the job you did on the Jones proposal." Or you could say, "You did an excellent job on the Jones proposal." Both are ways of recognizing the employee's work. But the second phrasing, beginning "You," will make a more positive impression.

It's a fact of human nature: we're essentially self-centered. If you could choose between talking about me and talking about you, which would you rather do? If you're like most people, you'd prefer to talk about you. Recognizing this preference, when possible convert "I" to "you." For example:

- Reword "I need a favor ..." to "You'd be doing me a favor if ..."
- Reword "I have a good idea ..." to "You may like this idea ..."
- Reword "I've increased productivity ..." to "You'll be pleased to know productivity ..."
- Reword "I've enclosed ..." to "You'll find enclosed ..."

Once you get the knack of it, you'll find it's easy to do. And it does make a difference in how people perceive you. You'll be seen as someone interested in them—their interests, their needs, their concerns—and that's very appealing to people.

The one exception to changing "I" to "you" is when you give corrective feedback, which is covered in Chapter 5.

Vocal Cues

How often do we speak without consciously considering how our voice sounds and the impression it makes on the people we're talking to? We ought to pay more attention to it. According to research by Dr. Albert Mehrabian, an expert on interpersonal communication, vocal cues account for more than a third of the meaning in a message when you talk to people face to face. It's even more when you talk on the telephone.

You may think, "This is the voice I was born with. It's how I sound and there's nothing I can do about." Not true. Like all communication cues, many vocal characteristics also are learned. If you notice a characteristic you'd like to change or improve, you can do it. Your voice is like a musical instrument. You can learn to "play" it in various ways.

Vocal characteristics include:

- Rate of speech
- Pitch
- Volume
- Tone

These are sometimes influenced by external factors, like time frame, setting, and the manner of the person you're com-municating with. If you've been given only five minutes to state your case, you may feel pressured to speed up the rate and talk faster than you normally do. If you're in noisy surroundings, you may raise the volume of your voice and speak louder than you normally do. If you're interacting with someone who's behaving in a way that's stressful or frustrating for you, you may react with a tone of voice you don't normally use.

It's understandable. But often it's not smart. Skilled, effective communicators take care to influence circumstances rather than be influenced by them. Bear in mind: your objective is to favorably influence what the other person perceives. You do that, in part, by managing the vocal cues you convey.

Let's consider common perceptions of various vocal characteristics.

Rate of Speech

When someone speaks at a rapid rate, what do you perceive? They're nervous. This is especially true if you know thepersonusuallydoesn'tracethroughtheirwordslikethey'redoing now. And "now" is when they're giving their first presentation in front of all of their peers. Of course they're nervous. But speeding up speech to get quickly through a stressful situation projects nervousness, which undermines your credibility.

Speaking quickly can also be taken to mean you're in a hurry. Of course you're in a hurry. You have more to do than time in which to do it all andyouhaven'tgotthetimetotalkwhenyouhavemoreimportantthingstodo.

If you're talking with someone in as much of a hurry as you are, speaking swiftly may be OK if you're both talking that way and if you both understand why you're doing it. But when someone comes to you with an issue they want to discuss, a rapid rate of speech sends the message, "I haven't got time for you."

Does building bridges of good employee relationships matter to you? Then make the time. Slow down your speech to the rate of casual conversation. Or schedule to meet with them later (but not too much later).

Here's another drawback to speaking rapidly. Did you notice the two occurrences of words strung together without spaces?

thepersonusuallydoesn'tracethroughtheirwordslikethey'redoing
andyouhaven'tgotthetimetotalkwhenyouhavemoreimportantthingstodo

Those aren't formatting errors. It was done deliberately to illustrate a point.

Did you find those lines more difficult to read? The spaces between written words are like the breaths and pauses between spoken words. Rapid speech is more difficult to listen to. Listeners will either give up and tune out or they may miss some of the meaning in your message.

What about a laboriously s-l-o-o-o-w rate of speech? It may be taken to mean the speaker's a slow thinker. Again, that may not be true, in fact. But when someone seems to be straining to get through a statement, often people perceive they're struggling to think.

Speaking slowly and carefully enunciating every word is perceived to be patronizing or condescending. Some people get the impression the speaker is "talking down" to them and they don't like it.

Pitch

The term "pitch" is borrowed from music. It denotes the degree to which a sound is high or low. A high-pitched sound is thinner than a lower one. In the extreme, it sounds squeaky or shrill. A low-pitched sound is fuller, more resonant. In the extreme, it's guttural, sounding somewhat like a growl.

A high-pitched voice is commonly associated with immaturity. Why? Because the young of every species vocalize at a high pitch. Baby birds peep, puppies yip, and children speak at a higher pitch than most adults.

What about a low-pitched voice? It can sound gruff. People who speak at a very deep pitch and low volume may be perceived to be mumbling or angry.

Overall, people tend to associate vocal qualities with personal qualities. A firm and resonant voice creates the perception of a steady, mature personality. Vocal power conveys strength of character. We know that's not always true in fact, but it is a common perception.

Volume

You may adjust the volume of your voice to adapt to a particular situation. When speaking one on one in close quarters, it's appropriate to lower the volume of your voice. If you're talking to a group of people in a large meeting room (without benefit of a microphone), you'd raise the volume of your voice in order to be heard by everyone.

In normal circumstances, talking loudly is unnecessary and may be perceived as harsh. Shouting is considered aggressive. The remark, "Don't raise your voice with me," is a defense against perceived aggression. On the other hand, someone who is soft-spoken is likely to be perceived as timid or shy.

Tone of Voice

Have you noticed how you quickly form an impression of a person from their tone of voice? It's one of the strongest nonverbal cues. Tone can have the effect of putting people at ease or putting them on guard.

Tones that put people on guard fuel negative perceptions. They include:

- Whining
- Defensive tone
- Aggressive tones: demanding, antagonistic, menacing
- Sarcastic tone

What do you perceive when a person speaks to you in a whiny tone? That you're being put upon. In a defensive tone? Their walls are up and you can't deal openly and honestly with them. Aggressive tones? You have no options or this is someone to be especially watchful of. What about a sarcastic tone of voice? You question, is that a put-down or what? You're not sure how to take it.

Although how each tone is perceived varies, in general they all cause the same effects. They're grating. They rub people the wrong way. And they leave you feeling boxed in. You'd prefer to

---

Curb the Sarcasm

Unfortunately, sarcasm is all too common these days. It's unfortunate because sarcasm undermines trust. As you may recall from Chapter 1, trust is one of the foundations of constructive communication.

Sarcasm undermines trust because people aren't sure what's meant by a sarcastic comment. Derogatory remarks that demean people are often said sarcastically. And criticism is often veiled in a sarcastic tone.

Some people say things sarcastically as a form of humor. If you do, do so only when there's a high degree of trust between you and the person you're joking with. And be sure your humorous intent is evident. Laugh when you say it.

communicate in a reasonable manner, but the person who habitually speaks in negative tones doesn't give you much of a chance. For these reasons, such tones almost always provoke a reaction.

There's an important lesson in this for managers. Watch *your* tone of voice. If you convey negative tones when you talk with employees, some will take it as license to do the same. Then you've really got problems on your hands when interactions among the work group are riddled with whining, defensiveness, aggression, and sarcastic sniping. It's not a pretty picture. It's also counterproductive.

How You Want to Sound

In most situations, the vocal quality you want to project is moderate with variations. "Moderate" means that your rate of speech is neither too fast nor too slow; the pitch is neither too high nor too low; the volume is neither too loud nor too soft; your tone of voice is reasonable, calm, and composed. In other words, the sound of your voice strikes a balance between extremes.

Of course, if you sustained that same balance beginning to end, you'd be speaking in a monotone, which lulls people to sleep. That's the purpose of adding variations.

Vary the rate, pitch, volume, and tone of your voice appropriately. Modulate your voice to add meaning to your message. Vary your voice to inject expressiveness. At times, it's most appropriate to sound empathetic. Other times, you'll express emphasis. Sometimes you'll rev it up to project enthusiasm and energy.

When you want to really drive a point home, here's a vocal technique that alerts the listener to sit up, take notice, and pay attention. Ever so subtly, lower the pitch, slow the rate, speak more softly when you make the point—then pause .... (A moment of silence.)

Visual Cues

You've no doubt heard the expression, "A picture's worth a thousand words." When you interact with people face to face,

---

Learn from the Pros

Have you ever been spellbound listening to a speaker? If so, you know a voice is a powerful thing. Most of us have potential in our voices we haven't begun to explore. Almost anyone can expand their vocal qualities and capabilities.

If your budget allows, you may consider hiring a voice coach. If not, take advantage of the many "voice coaches" you can learn from for free: broadcast journalists on TV. Channel surf and listen to several. Choose one or two whose voices appeal to you. Listen to how they use their voices in terms of rate, pitch, tone, and inflections. To practice improving your vocal qualities, emulate what they do. For the nominal cost of a seminar or audiotape, you can learn from professional speakers, too.

---

you present a picture to them by the visual cues you convey. Every nod, every gesture, a raised eyebrow, a smile, or a frown—everything you do sends a signal that makes an impression on your listener (who, by the way, is a viewer, too).

Some signals are so subtle most people don't consciously notice them. Others are obvious and have a significant impact on people's perceptions of you and your message. With some visual cues, the associated meanings differ from one culture to another. The descriptions that follow highlight the more obvious visual cues and what they generally indicate in North America.

Facial Expressions

To build bridges of constructive communications, you must appear approachable. Smile. Relax your face and look like you like what you do. A smile, coupled with a good-natured sense of humor, ranks high among likability factors. And you want people to like dealing with you.

Notice I didn't say, "like you, personally." Most good managers echo what you probably already know. As a manager, it's unlikely you'll take top prize in a popularity contest. But you do want people feeling they can come to you, that they can place their confidence in you, that you're agreeable to deal with even if you and they don't always agree.

Congruent Cues

In a private conversation, an employee relates a serious concern. The manager smiles broadly and says, "Yes, I understand your concern," as she shakes her head from side to side in a manner that signifies "No." What's wrong with this picture?

Leading a motivational meeting, the manager stands rigidly behind the lectern, brow furrowed as he looks down at his notes trying to make them out in the dim light. With head bowed as he reads from his notes, in a tone devoid of expression he says, "I'm very excited about the many awards this group has earned. It's been a great year. You've done a terrific job." What's wrong with this picture?

In these scenarios, the managers sent mixed messages. A message gets mixed when the cues don't coincide. Incongruent cues detract from your credibility and sometimes leave people feeling confused—or amused at your expense.

To make your meaning clear and increase its impact, convey vocal and visual cues that are consistent with the verbal words you say.

There are times, of course, when a smile is not appropriate. A goofy grin and giggling out of context rarely are. But there are many occasions throughout the day when we could smile and don't.

We get preoccupied with the problems. We've got our heads buried in the books. We're mesmerized by the monitor in front of us. We're doing many things at once and unaware of the grim expression of concentration frozen on our face. And it can put people off, making them feel unwelcome, ill at ease, or that maybe they ought to be as grim about this job as you appear to be. So remember:

- Show up at work with a smile on your face. Aren't you glad to be here? If you're not (or don't appear to be), why should employees be?
- Smile graciously when you greet people: when you pass them in the hallway or welcome them into your office or enter a meeting room.
- Smile broadly when someone gives you good news.
- Smile warmly when you recognize someone for good performance.

You also want to appear attentive. Make focused and meaningful eye contact when you interact with someone.

It's not fixing your eyes on people with an unrelenting stare. *Focused* eye contact refers to making their presence the focal point of your attention, generally looking eye to eye but occasionally glancing away for relief. *Meaningful* contact implies that your eyes reflect the meaning in your message when you're talking or, when the other person is talking, your eyes reflect your understanding of what they're telling you.

Refrain from eye movements that send a negative message. When interacting with others, don't roll your eyes as if to say, "Oh, brother," like you're bothered or disgusted. Don't glance around quickly with a shifty-eyed expression that suggests you can't be trusted.

Refrain from staring at the ceiling or down at your desk for any length of time. You may be deep in thought about what someone is telling you, but staring elsewhere conveys that you're bored or preoccupied with something else.

Head Movements

Nodding your head up and down signals, "Yes." Nod: Yes, I agree. Nod: Yes, that's right. Nod: Yes, that's a good idea. Shaking your head side to side signals, "No."

Many people nod as they listen. And the speaker perceives, "Great, they agree with me." Be careful that you don't unconsciously send a signal you don't mean.

Imagine I'm an employee you manage. I say, "Boss, I've been working really hard. I deserve a raise. I know I got a big pay increase three months ago, but the company's making lots of money. They should share the wealth. I'd like stock options, too, and while we're on the subject ..." Assume that while I've been talking, you've been nodding. Either you weren't aware you were nodding or you meant to convey, "I'm listening." What do I perceive? I think you've agreed with everything I've said. Now I'm excited because I'm going to get that raise. Oops, misperception created by your visual cue.

Here's another possible misperception. While someone's talking to you, refrain from shaking your head from side to side, which signals, "No." The person talking to you may perceive you've already made up your mind without giving them a chance to fully state their case.

Don't send what you don't intend. When you listen, keep your head still.

Gestures

Appropriate gestures express visually what you say verbally, so they serve to reinforce your message. An animated manner that punctuates points with gestures can help to sustain people's interest and attention.

Gestures can also detract from what you say. If you gesture too much or too expansively, the movement of hands and arms overwhelms your words. And some gestures have negative connotations. These are gestures you want to avoid.

- Don't point at people. Pointing a finger in someone's face is perceived as parental, accusatory, or dictatorial. It's offensive. If you point to add emphasis, find another way. Use intonations. Gesture to the side with an open palm. Or with both hands open in front of you, gently strike the palm of one hand with the edge of the other.
- Don't wring your hands or fiddle with items like your watch, a ring, your tie or scarf, your collar, earrings, or objects on your desk. Such gestures give the impression that you're nervous or impatient. You may be, but don't let on that you are.
- Refrain from dismissive, disrespectful, or aggressive gestures, like "waving away" someone's idea or pounding your fist on the desk. Those kinds of gestures are sure to trigger negative perceptions and reactions.

Sitting and Standing

Whether you're seated or standing, you want to convey the impression that you're alert, so keep your posture upright. An upright posture also projects and sustains greater energy. At the

Neutralize Negativity

If you happen to interact with someone who's a negative thinker, moderate your communications accordingly. Be especially cautious about the verbal, vocal, and visual cues you convey. Negativity is a high-intensity state of mind and emotion. As you may have discovered, it doesn't take much to set it off. Negative thinkers are easily provoked and typically exhibit reactionary behavior.

To reduce the occurrence of negative reactions:

1. Keep your cues neutral. Drain the emotion and expressiveness out of your words, tone of voice, and gestures. Appear impassive, unruffled by their reactions. Use a flat, but firm, tone of voice.
2. Don't get drawn in and react to their negative cues. Don't argue. Why not? You can't win.
3. Encourage dialogue. Use questions that seek their input.
4. Listen attentively. Often, negative thinkers feel they're not being heard, which exacerbates their negativity.
5. State clearly the boundaries of appropriate workplace behavior. If you find a negative thinker's behavior is infecting the work group (which it typically does), confront it. Give them corrective feedback. (See Chapter 5.)

same time, you want to appear confident and at ease, not rigid. A rigid posture projects tension or formality.

When sitting in the presence of others, don't sit back or slump too casually in your chair. The perception is that you're disinterested, indifferent, or taking casually the subject of discussion.

When you want to emphasize a point or signify heightened interest in what the other person is saying, lean forward slightly. But don't lean so far forward that you appear to be "in their face."

Spatial Relationship

This has to do with the space that exists between you and a person you're talking to. It's an aspect of interpersonal communication that differs from one person to another. We all have a preference as to the space that represents our comfort zone. It also differs from one culture to another.

As a rule, don't intrude on another person's space. Respect their comfort zone. When in doubt, take your cue from them. Or leave a "handshake's distance." This is the amount of space that would be between the two of you if you approached one another to shake hands.

When you approach someone who's seated, sit down, too, so you can converse at eye level. Standing over someone who's seated can create the impression you're intimidating.

Attire

What you wear is a visual cue. Does your attire send the message that you're clean, well-groomed, a professional who makes a favorable impression? Or does it convey the impression that you're slovenly and couldn't care less about how people perceive you?

What are the norms in your organization? Is it customary for managers to wear suits, except on "casual Friday"? Or is casual attire the norm all week?

Surroundings

Do you expect employees to keep their work areas clean and orderly? Many companies do, especially in areas that are visible to the public. The appearance of the working environment sends visual cues, too.

How does *your* office look? If your desk and credenza and file cabinets and floor are littered with paperwork and binders and such, what message does that send to employees? And what might your boss perceive?

What's Appropriate Attire?

If you're in doubt about how to dress in your workplace, look "two up." Check out the attire worn by managers or executives who are two levels up the organization from you. If you have career aspirations to achieve that same or a higher level, you want to foster the perception that you're "like them."

This doesn't mean spending exorbitant amounts of money on the exclusive brand labels they may buy. It doesn't mean copycatting their every mannerism. It means adopting, overall, an executive style that suggests you're a promotable person well-suited to occupy a higher office.

No Matter What You Do ...

Of course, no matter what you do, there will still be occasions when some people misperceive you or misinterpret what you say. On the upside, you can reduce those occurrences by managing your output. As you've seen, all of the cues you convey to others influence their perceptions—and you can make it a positive influence.

Now let's consider the second aspect of managing perceptions.

Managing Your Perceptions

Switch roles. In this section, you're in the role of *perceiver*. Imagine you're in a conversation with an employee, your boss, or a colleague. Based on what they say and do, you form perceptions. Are they always accurate?

Throughout this chapter, you've seen examples of how perceptions may differ from what's true in fact. You don't want possible misperceptions clouding your judgment. So before you act, respond, or react based on your perceptions, manage them.

Gather the Facts

You have a vacancy to fill in your department. You've narrowed the applicants to five you'll interview. The third candidate you talk with has excellent interview skills. She's articulate and projects a professional demeanor. She exudes enthusiasm and a can-do attitude. By the end of the interview, you're so impressed you're ready to offer her the job on the spot. STOP.

Have you done a background check? Have you talked with the people she listed as references? Have you compared her résumé against those of other candidates, including the two you haven't interviewed yet? Has she completed the pre-employment testing you normally require after the interview stage? If the answer to any of those questions is "No," you don't have all the facts.

This interview scenario is just one example of the many decisions you make. In personnel matters alone, you make decisions about employee development, delegation of tasks and projects, recognition, discipline, promotion, and termination.

The best decision is the most informed decision. Going with first impressions or your personal perceptions is like letting your heart rule over your head. That may be fine in romance, but it's not fitting for business. To make wise and fair decisions—and to be perceived as someone who does—get the facts and assess them with discernment.

Solicit Input from Others

Sandy comes to you with a complaint about Marty, who works in another department across the hall. You've heard a rumor or two that Marty is difficult to get along with. You like Sandy. She brings you coffee in the morning. She picks up your dry cleaning. And she does her job fairly well, too. So you perceive Sandy's right.

You're ready to head across the hall and let Marty's supervisor know in no uncertain terms that you won't stand for people from that department upsetting your employees. STOP. You don't have all the facts. And you haven't talked with anyone else to verify Sandy's story.

Find out from other people what they perceive to be true. When others are involved or will be affected by a decision you make, ask them questions to learn how they see the situation. The insights you gain help you refine your perceptions and expand your perspective.

Separate Perceptions from Performance

Have you found there are some people you have a natural affinity with, and one or two others who grate on your nerves? You don't know why exactly; they just do. There's something about them you perceive negatively.

Our perceptions about a person tend to influence how we assess their performance. Negative perceptions can obscure our view of the positive things they do. Likewise, positive perceptions about a person cast a rosy hue over what they do, even when they do something that ought to be corrected.

Take care to distinguish between your perceptions of a person and the facts of their performance. If you harbor unfavorable impressions of a person, don't automatically dismiss their ideas, which may have merit. Don't discount the results they produce. With people you perceive positively, do your best to evaluate their ideas and performance objectively. Remember the advice of Peter Drucker: "Effective executives never ask, 'How well does he get along with me?' Their question is 'What does he contribute?'" (*The Effective Executive*, Harper & Row, 1967).

Clarify by Perception Checking

Sometimes a person communicates a cue and you're uncertain how to interpret it. Or you find it bothersome or disturbing. Before you react, check your perception.

Perception checking is easy to do. It consists of:

- Observation: state what you observed
- Impression: give your impression, your interpretation
- Clarification: find out the meaning of the observed behavior

Here's how it sounds.

After a meeting, you take Joe aside and say, "I noticed you rolled your eyes when I suggested we cover the tech line on a rotational basis. I have the impression you think it's a bad idea. Is that right?" Joe may say, "Yeah, it's a bad idea." Now the issue's out in the open and you can discuss it. Or, he may say something like "No, I think your idea's OK. I was annoyed because Paul kept interrupting with all those questions." His explanation corrects your misperception.

In some instances, you don't state your impression outright because you don't want to appear to be jumping to conclusions. First, you want to hear what the other person has to say. For example: "I hear what sounds like a tone of frustration. What's that about?" Take care to ask in a moderate tone of voice so you don't come across sounding defensive.

Perception checking serves to:

- Avoid unnecessary misunderstandings
- Convey your interest in or concern for the other person

- Hold people accountable for their communication behaviors

A Useful Self-Assessment

Recognizing the impact and influence of perceptions, *consciously* reflect on questions that help increase your awareness of what you do.

With respect to your perceptions, periodically consider: What is my impression of this person? of this situation? What factors have produced this perception? Is it an accurate impression?

To better manage other people's perceptions, ask yourself: How do I want to be perceived by this person (or these people) in this situation? This question is especially important to consider before you go into high-stakes situations, such as giving an employee their performance review, a presentation before your peers or upper management, your performance review with your boss.

At the least, you want to be perceived as confident, competent, and a constructive communicator. So ask yourself: What do I need to say and do to foster that favorable view? This question helps you identify communication skills you may

Three Critical Questions

For Example

If you're a fan of football, you're probably familiar with college coach Lou Holtz. He achieved national prominence when, as head coach at Notre Dame, he led the team to 10 consecutive winning seasons and the 1988 National Championship with a perfect record.

Holtz points out that before people willingly accept and eagerly respond to your leadership, they have in mind three questions.
- Can I trust you?
- Are you committed to excellence?
- Do you care about me?

It isn't enough for you to answer those questions verbally. People arrive at the answers themselves by what they perceive to be true of you. So periodically assess what you project and the manner in which you interact with people.

want to improve.

The Communicator's Checklist for Chapter 2

❑ Keep in mind the power of perceptions.

❑ Convey verbal, vocal, and visual cues that contribute to constructive communications and prompt positive responses from people. Refrain from those that are likely to provoke negative reactions.

❑ Manage your perceptions by getting facts and inviting input from others. Maintain your objectivity and check your perceptions of what other people do.

❑ Develop and consistently apply the interpersonal skills that promote positive perceptions of you.

Profiles and Preferences

No one would talk much in society if he knew how often he
misunderstands others.
—Johann Wolfgang von Goethe

Seek first to understand ...
—Stephen Covey

Imagine you're leading a meeting attended by every member
of your team. Your boss is sitting in on the meeting, too.
You're standing at the front of the conference room. Look
around. Notice every person seated around the table. What do
you see? A skillful communicator will spot the variety of communication profiles present in the group.

You've undoubtedly discovered that no two people communicate alike. If we were all on the same wavelength, we'd have
few of the problems that occur as a consequence of break-
downs in communication. When communication breaks down,
usually it can be traced to differing *perceptions* (discussed in the
preceding chapter) or to differing *profiles*.

Do you find some people more difficult to deal with than
others? In some cases, a behavior we consider difficult isn't

truly *difficult*. It's *different*. When you understand the other person's profile and adapt your communication to it, you'll experience fewer difficulties. You'll be

> **Profile** In the context of interpersonal communication, the traits and tendencies a person exhibits when they express themselves and interact with others.

more effective in getting your message across. And the outcomes of your dealings with people will be more successful.

A profile consists of two factors:

- communication style
- thought pattern

Although these may vary somewhat depending on the circumstances and who we're communicating with, we're inclined to favor one style and pattern.

Communication Styles

If you've read about or attended courses on communication skills, you're probably familiar with the terms that are commonly used to describe communication styles. This may be a review for you. If so, it's a useful review as a preface to understanding the profiles.

As you read through the explanations that follow, picture the styles appearing along a scale that looks like this:

Passive	Expressive	Aggressive

Figure 3-1. A continuum of communication styles

Aggressive

This style appears at one end of the scale, indicating it's excessive. It exceeds the bounds of reasonable behavior. In terms of communication cues, aggressive communicators typically speak at high volume and at a high (shrieking) or low (growling) pitch. Their tone of voice tends to be demanding or sarcastic.

Aggressive communication is forceful, contentious, even bombastic. It's an "in your face" type of communication. Someone who's not aggressive perceives it as intimidating. Someone else who's aggressive perceives it as an invitation to do battle verbally. (And you hope it doesn't go any further than a *verbal* contest.)

Aggressive communicators don't thoughtfully respond. They react, often with anger or with an intimidating demeanor. They convey the impression that they, and they alone, are right. Therefore, they tend to monopolize a conversation and rarely listen without interrupting. As a result, an aggressive style doesn't lend itself to mutual exchange. The phrase "meaningful dialogue" isn't in their vocabulary.

Passive

At the opposite end of the scale, this style is also an extreme. It's extremely submissive. Passive communicators assume a subordinate role, even if their position in the organization isn't a subordinate one. They subordinate themselves when interacting with others. They tend to give in or back off quickly, especially when confronted by an aggressive communicator.

Generally, passive communicators speak at a low volume, sometimes so softly it sounds as if they're mumbling. Their tone of voice is timid and deferential. Often, they avoid eye contact.

You might think an aggressive style is more difficult to deal with than a passive one. That's not always the case. Because passive communicators are acquiescent, it can be difficult to discern what they think. In a group discussion, they're reluctant to bring up their ideas. As a result, you may miss the benefit of some good ones.

Ask their opinion and they'll say they agree with you, even if they really don't. Ask if they have time to work on a task, they'll say, "Yes" to please you and passively accept more assignments than they can handle. As a result, some tasks get done late, carelessly, or not at all.

Because this style is the opposite of aggressive, you might think a passive communicator listens, unlike an aggressive one.

Again, that's not always the case. They might appear to be passively listening when, in fact, they've retreated into their own thoughts. And because they rarely convey verbal, vocal, or visual feedback, you have no indication of whether they're really listening or not.

Like aggressive communicators, passives also tend to react. Rather than speaking up in a reasonable manner, some shut down. Like a turtle pulling its head into its shell, they withdraw. If you ask them, "What's wrong?" they mutter, "Nothing." Others complain or whine. They think complaining is the only way they'll get heard or they've learned from experience that whining gets them what they want.

Passive-Aggressive

As the term implies, this style is a hybrid of the first two. It's essentially passive. The passive communicator takes it, takes it, takes it, and takes some more. Finally, they get filled up—with frustration, resentment, and the stress of having suppressed their feelings. Once they get all filled up, they're going to get even. They *react.*

The pendulum swings to the opposite end of the scale and they react aggressively. It can be difficult to interact with this style because it's unpredictable. From one day to the next, you're never quite sure what to expect.

Expressive

This style is commonly referred to as *assertive.* Since "assertive" is often confused with "aggressive," I prefer the term "expressive." It's a synonym for "assertive" and better describes the nature of this style.

It appears in the middle of the scale because it's a well-balanced style. Neither brashly aggressive nor submissively passive, an expressive communicator speaks up. They express their ideas. They voice their concerns. They make their interests known. And they do it in a moderate manner: at a moderate volume, pitch, and conversational rate of speech, and with an appropriately modulated tone of voice. They're candid without being confrontational or complaining.

They understand the prefix "di" in "dialogue" means "two." They've learned the most effective communication is two-way. So they not only express themselves; they give others an opportunity to express themselves, too. Seeking to understand, they listen attentively. They ask questions and express interest in others to encourage a mutual exchange.

Generally, expressive communicators respond reasonably. If confronted by an aggressive communicator, they refrain from lashing back. Instead, they'll do their best to maintain their composure and bring calm to the interaction. When dealing with a passive communicator, they'll do their best to draw them out and involve them in the conversation.

Thought Patterns

You've probably heard reference to right-brain and left-brain thinking. You may be familiar with the theory of multiple intelligences. If you follow the news, you're aware that research continues to discover more about the way our minds work. In view of the diversity among human beings and the complexity of the brain, the following discussion isn't concerned with all possible patterns and permutations of thought.

For our purposes—to identify communication profiles—we're going to focus on two primary patterns of thought: concrete and conceptual. Although some people think equally well in both ways, most of us have a propensity for one or the other.

At Your Wit's End?

At times, you may find the communication behaviors of passive and aggressive styles bring you to the brink of reacting. You may feel frustrated, irritated, even angry. If so, before you react, remove yourself from the situation. Temporarily retreat in order to regroup and to let emotions subside—theirs and yours.

Say something generic like "Let's give this more thought before we continue." Do not say something like "You need to calm down." It sounds like you're pointing the finger of blame at them, which will provoke a real reaction!

Concrete Thinking

The core of concrete thinking is logic and a tendency to view and interpret things literally. Concrete thought proceeds sequentially: *A* leads to *B*, which leads to *C*. Follow the sequence and you'll reach a logical conclusion. (When a concrete thinker relates aloud this kind of thought pattern, a conceptual thinker says, "You're missing my point." You'll see why when you get to Conceptual Thinking.)

A concrete thinker applies this same linear logic to problem solving. They identify the particulars of a problem to diagnose the root cause. They take a pragmatic approach, dissect the various parts, and solve the problem systematically.

Like Sergeant Friday on the old television series, *Dragnet*, concrete thinkers want "just the facts." They like to deal with data, figures, and specifics. They use, and respond best to, informational language that conveys just the facts without extraneous explanations or drawn-out descriptions. They tend to focus on function.

They enjoy building *things*. Concrete thinkers talk in terms of *think, analyze, calculate, devise, parameters* and *practical details*—because that's what you're concerned with when you build things.

Conceptual Thinking

At the heart of conceptual thinking is intuition and imagination. Conceptual thought plays through the mind circuitously. *A* sounds like *K*, which, if you close the top, calls to mind an image of *R*. Skirt around the circuit at random and you'll produce a creative idea. (When a conceptual thinker expresses aloud this kind of thought pattern, a concrete thinker says, "What?!")

A conceptual thinker brings this creative process and "gut feelings" to problem solving. They look at the "big picture" and ponder various possibilities. An innovative solution evolves—or not. In their view, how you feel about the solution matters as much as the solution itself.

As the term *concept* implies, conceptual thinkers value ideas and theories. The abstract appeals to them. They use, and respond best to, relational language that is emotive and descriptive. Verbal illustrations, imagery, and metaphors appeal to them. They view things as fluid rather than fixed, and value form over function.

They enjoy building *relationships*. They talk in terms of *feel, sense, experience, insights, impressions,* and *emotions*—because that's what you're interested in when you build relationships.

A Matter of Misunderstanding

Suppose you're a concrete thinker. I've returned from lunch and you ask me, "How's the weather?" You're not interested in making idle conversation. You're concerned with making a decision. Because it was raining when you came to work this morning, you're trying to decide whether to take your umbrella when you go to lunch.

If I'm a conceptual thinker, I'll say something like this: "It's sunny. And I love it when the sun shines because it lifts my spirits and the warmth reminds me of days on the beach when I went to Hawaii on vacation. I just love Hawaii. Don't you?"

If you're a concrete thinker, what do you think? *Why are you babbling?!* All you need to know, factually, is what the weather is like. I didn't mean to come across as babbling. I described and disclosed as much as I did to be friendly and so develop our working relationship.

Suppose you're a conceptual thinker. You ask me, "How's the weather?" If I'm a concrete thinker, I'll reply in purely practical terms, "It's sunny (period)." How do you feel? You feel like I reacted abruptly, meaning that either I don't have time for you or I'm rude. I didn't mean to sound rude. I said what I logically concluded was all that you needed to answer your question. The concrete thinker figures if you want to know more, you'll ask more.

This example points out how people can misunderstand one another, even in a seemingly simple situation, because of differing patterns of thought. The potential for misunderstanding and strained working relationships becomes even greater when you add to these thought patterns the communication styles and come up with four different profiles.

Communication Profiles

The following diagram depicts the settings in which you interact with others: your workplace, professional and social situations, your household. View this as is your "world" and it's populated with various personalities.

In the diamond shape at the center, you find people who interact in a reasonable manner. Naturally, we experience differences in the way we think and communicate. But as long as we don't go to extremes, we're in the diamond. We understand, accommodate, and adapt to one another so differences don't erupt into difficulties or divisiveness.

You'll notice the diagram is divided into four quadrants, one for each communication profile.

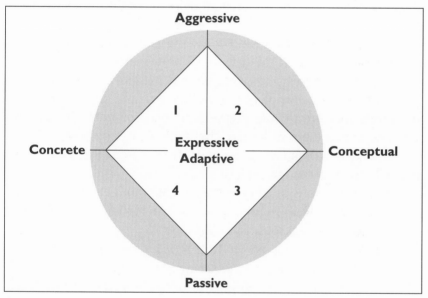

Figure 3-2.

The vertical axis refers to communication styles. Within the diamond, these range from moderately expressive at the center up to a more highly expressive style: animated, exuberant, or extroverted. From the center, the degree of expressiveness decreases to a mild-mannered style: less forthright, more reserved, sometimes introspective.

People in the upper half, in quadrants 1 and 2, tend to respond quickly. They make decisions quickly. They adapt to change quickly. Occasionally they initiate change just because they're bored with the same old thing. Their motto is "Just Do It!"

People in the lower half, in quadrants 3 and 4, tend to be more cautious. Before making a decision, they deliberate. They need assurance it's the best decision. They're sometimes slow to accept change, preferring the status quo. As long as things remain the same, there are fewer decisions to consider and fewer unforeseen consequences. Their motto is "Look before you leap."

Thought patterns appear along the horizontal axis. As the term "adaptive" suggests, someone at the center can easily adjust their thinking. They appreciate and grasp equally well both the conceptual and the concrete. Moving from the center out to the right indicates an increasing degree of conceptual thinking; to the left, the pattern of thinking becomes increasingly concrete.

Extremes occur in the gray circle that surrounds the diamond. The extremes of aggressive and passive communications appear at the outer ends of the vertical axis. At one end of the horizontal axis are people whose thinking is so conceptual you can't convince them to look at the facts. At the opposite end are those whose thinking is so concrete they can't see the proverbial forest for the trees.

Understandably, such extremes create conflicts and can disrupt teamwork. They're among the counterproductive communication behaviors discussed in Chapter 6.

For now, let's focus on the four profiles that appear in the diamond zone of reasonable interactions. As you read through the descriptions, call to mind the employees you manage and other people you work with. See if you can determine the predominant profile of each.

Profile 1: *Movers & Shakers*
Communication Style: moderately to highly expressive
Thought Pattern: adaptive to concrete

Movers & Shakers are primarily motivated to achieve goals. Sometimes described as "Drivers," they are driven to succeed. They focus on producing short-term results to achieve their long-range objectives and fulfill their mission. They view setbacks and obstacles as challenges. If they perceive something

> ## No Pigeon-Holing, Please
> **⚠ CAUTION!**
>
> Each profile here is identified by a *title* that appears in italic type. These titles are concepts meant solely to convey a chief characteristic of the profile they name. They are *not* intended to label people.
>
> Bear in mind what you know from experience. People are not only and always one way. In one situation you may appear to be predominantly one type. In a different situation, you may shift your orientation and adopt a different profile.
>
> The purpose of profiling is *not* to pigeon-hole people. It's to gain insights that give us a greater understanding of ourselves and others. With that understanding, we gain ideas of how to adapt our communications.

or someone is getting in their way, they press ahead with even more persistence.

They prefer to be in charge. It's understandable. Being in charge gives them greater control so they can "muster the troops" and direct resources to progress toward their goals.

Although it isn't always the case, people tend to be drawn to professions that appeal to their communication style and thought pattern. They gravitate to occupations that allow them to satisfy their primary motivator. As the term *Movers & Shakers* implies, people in positions of leadership generally appear in this quadrant: executives, managers, directors, and entrepreneurs. People in uniform often appear here, too: military officers, police officers, and firefighters, for example. A uniform and brass or a badge are symbols of being in charge. And all of these positions require someone who's decisive, especially in crisis, and who's sufficiently assertive to give orders without hesitation.

Another of the clues to a person's profile is the objects they have around them in their surroundings. With *Movers & Shakers* you'll see "trophies"—tangible evidence of the goals they've achieved. You'll notice on their walls awards of recognition, commendation letters, photographs of them at prestigious events or in the company of higher-ups. A trophy from a golf or tennis tournament may grace their credenza.

Communication cues offer additional clues. *Movers &
Shakers* think and talk in terms of "the bottom line." They use
expressions like "get to the point," "net it out," and "cut to the
chase." Vocally, their voice may come across as clipped, even
curt. They may snap their fingers, glance at their watch, or display similar visual signals of impatience. They don't intend to
offend. They're just preoccupied with getting on with it so they
can get back to work on their goals.

Profile 2: *Narrators*
Communication Style: highly to moderately expressive
Thought Pattern: conceptual to adaptive

In this quadrant, you'll find people who are primarily motivated by a desire to tell their story and be recognized for it.
When they were youngsters, they loved being called on to get
up in front of the class for "Show and Tell." They're energized
by an audience and relish applause. They're gratified by the
pure pleasure of performing well.

In a business context, their "story" is related to what they do
for a living. They're salespeople who tell you about their company, products, or services. Every prospect is a prospective
audience. The recognition they seek comes in the form of com-
missions, bonuses, sales awards, and a pat on the back.

They're front-line customer service reps who like dealing
with people and can live for a week off a "Thank you" note from

A Lesson from Andrew Carnegie

Andrew Carnegie was a consummate *Mover & Shaker*. From a
childhood of poverty, he achieved enough goals during his life-
time to become a leader of the Industrial Revolution, the richest man in
the world, and one of its most generous benefactors. When asked what
his greatest business asset was, he answered, "people." If you took away
his land and buildings and machinery, he said, but left him his people, he'd
get it all back again and more.

The lesson in this is not to become so driven to achieve goals that
we overlook the value of building relationships. Make time to gain
understanding and interact with good interpersonal skills so people
are eager to do their very best for you.

Ring the Bell!

In a company known for its stellar sales force, one region made recognition a top priority. Special events for salespeople and customer support staff were held quarterly, hosted by the regional manager. Awards were handed out monthly. In every branch office, a brass bell was installed. When someone brought in an order, large or small, the manager personally rang the bell. The region earned the award for national sales leader of the year.

"Ringing the bell" doesn't mean you do so literally (although you might). It means paying lots of attention—audibly and visibly—and especially doing so with your revenue producers. It means communicating motivating messages on a regular basis, not just during a once-a-year special event and not only for the big accomplishments.

---

a satisfied customer. They're trainers, teachers, public speakers, liberal arts professors, trial attorneys, and entertainers.

Often, you'll find that *Narrators* are self-motivated. Yes, they're motivated by applause and recognition, but they know they can't always count on getting it from others. So they have in their surroundings and keep close at hand items that sustain their self-motivation.

Their walls or desks are covered with posters and plaques with inspirational sayings. They keep a file of complimentary (preferably glowing) letters and reviews. They're in their element at special events, like sales conferences, where there's lots of hoopla to recognize them or their kind. Some read self-help and motivational books.

From their communication cues, it's relatively easy to spot a *Narrator*. They tend to be very verbal. They use analogies and metaphors and tell stories to get their message across. They're inclined to elaborate, embellishing points. In short, they're talkative.

Narrators tend to be colorful characters and creative. They're constantly coming up with what they think are bright ideas. In a discussion, they're likely to take off on tangents. You may think the tangent derails the discussion. They feel it's an interesting detour that ought to be explored because it may lead to an even brighter idea. "Brainstorming" ranks high on their list

TRICKS OF THE TRADE

Ssshhh ...

Does the profile of a *Narrator* fit you? If so, how would you rate your listening skills?

When you interact with people, think: if I listen closely, there's a chance I'll pick up something I can use the next time I have a story to tell. (This assumes, of course, that the person is not divulging anything confidential.) When you listen, you discover that many people (including those who aren't *Narrators*) have wonderful stories, amusing anecdotes, humorous expressions, profound insights, or useful information. When you're not listening, you're not learning. Think of listening as information-gathering research.

of favorite things to do, provided they can occupy center stage during the brainstorming session.

They're animated communicators who express themselves with multiple visual cues: lively facial expressions, expansive gestures, and body movement. *Narrators* who are in the public eye generally use a lot of inflection when they speak and project their voices well.

What they sometimes don't do well is listen. They don't mean to be rude or insensitive toward you. They're just so eager to tell their story they may not think to stop and hear yours.

Profile 3: *Care Givers*
Communication Style: mildly to moderately expressive
Thought Pattern: conceptual to adaptive

Care Givers are the "people persons" of the world. Their chief motivation is to serve others. What's in it for them? They gain satisfaction from doing something worthy of approval, something that fulfills their need to be needed.

They're involved in vocations that contribute significant value, not so much at an economic but at a human level. As the term implies, *Care Givers* take care of the rest of us. They're teachers, nurses, therapists, secretaries, administrative support personnel, day care workers, emergency medical technicians, rescue workers, counselors, and volunteers.

The objects in their surroundings reflect the relational and nurturing nature of *Care Givers*. You'll notice pictures of family, their children, their pets, and the staff at a birthday party they planned for a coworker. Often it's *Care Givers* who take the initiative to do things that forge social bonds among coworkers: organizing office parties, the company softball team, circulating special-occasion cards for everyone to sign.

They like plants in their work area. They tend to collect soft huggable stuffed toys, amusing trinkets, and angelic figurines. If you see someone wearing a happy-face button, chances are it's a *Care Giver*.

Their relational nature expresses itself in a conversational, self-disclosing style. They like a friendly chat because they see it as a way to build relationships. To a *Care Giver*, a question like "How's the weather?" is an invitation to get to know one another better.

Although they share with *Narrators* the conceptual pattern of thinking, their communication style is noticeably more mild-mannered. They're more soft-spoken, they use fewer gestures, and often the inflection in their voice ends on an upward note that makes a statement sound like a question. Unlike assertive communicators, they tend to be more reserved about stating a point.

Not wishing to offend, *Care Givers* tend toward the passive style. They may hesitate to speak up unless an issue really matters to them. They're reluctant to confront. Typically, they avoid conflict because it's upsetting to them. And they find it difficult to stand up to aggressive communicators.

They speak in terms that convey their desire to please, seeking approval with questions like "Is that OK with you?" They may hedge with remarks like "I'm not sure this is exactly what you wanted, but ..." And even when they haven't done anything to apologize for, the more passive personality may sound apologetic: "I'm sorry you didn't meet the deadline ...."

Profile 4: *Map Makers*
Communication Style: mildly to moderately expressive
Thought Pattern: concrete to adaptive

The term *Map Maker* applies to people who do what map makers do—they design and develop the things the rest of us

Acquire Critical Skills

Smart Managing   A registered nurse with an excellent performance record, Trina was promoted to shift supervisor. Within days, she was feeling the strain of complaints and conflicts employees brought to her. With little preparation for her new management role, Trina found herself facing issues that required more than care-giving skills.

You may be in such a situation yourself or you may manage people who are. In care-giving professions especially, it's not unusual to find a former *Care Giver* feels like they're in over their head when they become "manager."

The solution lies, at least in part, in training in assertiveness and conflict resolution skills. The relational and supportive nature of *Care Givers* makes them potentially effective managers. But they may not fulfill that potential if they don't learn how to assert themselves and step up to conflicts.

use. They are motivated to figure things out and fit them together. And they have a need to do it with absolute accuracy. They need assurance it's going to be right.

They're methodical, analytical, and meticulously attentive to detail. They tend to be problem solvers. As such, they're also motivated by the challenge of the process itself. They gain a great deal of satisfaction from finding "a fix" for the bug, the glitch, the seemingly insurmountable obstacle.

You'll find them in professions like accounting, architecture, engineering, computer programming, quality control, and mechanical or technical repair. They're science and math professors, technical writers, and scientific researchers.

What objects will you find in their surroundings? Computers, or course. Calculators. Rulers measured in metrics. Printouts and spreadsheets. (*Map Makers* love spreadsheets.) On a wall of their office or cubicle, you're likely to see a color-coded, year-at-a-glance planning calendar. They use mechanical pencils and fine-point pens in different colors. At home, their tools are meticulously organized on peg boards. Every object is selected and arranged to make it easier for them to do any job with the utmost accuracy.

Map Makers are predominantly concrete thinkers and appear at the lower end on the scale of expressiveness. By now, you can probably figure out the kind of communication to expect when you interact with a *Map Maker*. A *Map Maker* is a man or a woman of few words. When they talk, they show little interest in topics that are extraneous to the task at hand. They tend to be very task-focused.

They refer and respond best to facts, figures, data, and specific details. Ask them, "How's the weather?" and they'll tell you the temperature in both Fahrenheit and Celsius degrees. They prefer material in printed or written form. Refrain from using the word "assume" when talking with a *Map Maker*. In their view, no assumption is safe; no theory is true until tested and proven.

Their vocal and visual cues tend to be restrained, making it difficult to discern what a *Map Maker* really thinks. If you're an expressive communicator and excited about a project, your enthusiasm shows. You may interpret their quiet manner, in contrast, as a lack of enthusiasm. In fact, the *Map Maker* may be more enthused than you are. Usually, they just don't outwardly display how they feel.

The Ideal Team

Suppose your boss came to you and said, "I'm putting you in charge of this top-priority project. You can go throughout the organization and select any employees you want on your team." Who would you choose?

Often, we're inclined to pick people we perceive to be like us. As the saying goes, "Birds of a feather flock together."

If a *Mover & Shaker* picked for their team only employees who were *Movers & Shakers* what would happen? Not much, at least not much on the project. They'd get caught up in competing for the position of team leader and arguing over who sits at the head of the conference table. And the assertive communication styles of some would quickly escalate into aggression.

If a *Narrator* put together a team of like-minded *Narrators*, what would happen? Again, not much on the project. They'd

Reduce Disagreements and Delays

A common point of contention between *Map Makers* and their managers is the time it takes to complete a project. Charged with producing results, many managers want them *now*. Intent on producing as-perfect-as-possible results, *Map Makers* want more time.

• At the outset, clearly communicate, gain agreement on, and put in writing the end objective and specifications.
• Negotiate a reasonable time frame to produce the specified result.
• Develop a contingency plan.
• Throughout the course of the project, meet for follow-up and feedback at regular intervals to keep tabs on the pace and progress of the project.

spend time telling one another stories, taking off on tangents in project meetings, having bright ideas but not seeing them through to completion because another idea popped up.

What about a team of all *Care Givers*? In project meetings, they'd take time for coffee and doughnuts and friendly conversation. They'd compare photo albums. If someone had a birthday coming up, they'd postpone the project to plan the party.

It would seem, then, that the best team would consist of the task-focused *Map Makers*. But with a team made up solely of *Map Makers*, a project can suffer paralysis from over-analysis. And progress slows when they rework tasks to make things "perfect."

Although these scenarios are intended to be humorous, they serve to make a point. Clearly, the ideal team is one that includes employees of every type. No one profile owns the exclusive rights to peak performance. Each has shortcomings; each has strengths. Blending the different communication styles and thought patterns adds balance. Because you can capitalize on the strengths of each profile, a blended work group brings about the best results—*if* ...

If we understand one another in terms of profiles and preferences, and communicate accordingly, we can get past our differences and pull together.

How to Customize Your Communication

Chapter 1 introduced the ABCs of constructive communications. You may recall the "C" stood for "customize your communication to the person you're interacting with." To do so, you need to be flexible to adapt and apply some Dos and Don'ts when dealing with different profiles.

Interacting with Movers & Shakers

An astute manager will engage these goal-oriented employees in joint goal-setting sessions. When you discuss with them the goals and results you expect them to achieve, invite their input. Ask them what goals they have. Present the results you want in terms of "means to an end" for them. If, for example, they want to get promoted (a common goal for *Movers & Shakers*), show them how supporting your goals is a means to achieving theirs.

Talk to them about *strategies, action plans, progress, accomplishments,* and *solutions.* These are action words that appeal to *Movers & Shakers.*

Managing a *Mover & Shaker* is comparable to taming a wild horse. You don't want to break their spirit. You do want to show them who's in charge. They'll relate to and respect that.

Be decisive and speak to them in a firm tone of voice. If you tend to be a more mild-mannered communicator, adopt a more assertive manner with them. But stop short of coming across as harsh or controlling.

Remember: *Movers & Shakers* like to be in charge. Offer them options that allow them a degree of control. Delegate tasks or projects that give them opportunities to fill a leadership role, such as doing in-house training or mentoring other employees. When you do, make clear the limits of their authority and require that they report the results to you.

Don't waste their time. During meetings, have you noticed one or two employees who shift in their seats, glance at their watch, sigh with apparent impatience? They may be the *Movers & Shakers* of the group who think they have better things to do with their time, like getting back to work on their goals. When you

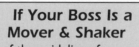

If Your Boss Is a Mover & Shaker

Most of the guidelines for interacting with a *Mover & Shaker* employee also apply to dealing with a boss of this type—except:

- Don't give the impression you're trying to take charge and take over.
- If you tend to be assertive, tone it down. Refrain from being confrontational.
- Show your support for the boss's goals. If you're not sure what they are, ask.
- Present your results in relation to their goals.

have meetings, look for items on the agenda you can ask them to present. Or periodically delegate leadership of meetings to them. And when you talk with them one on one, get to the point.

Be prepared. Do your homework. *Movers & Shakers* tend to be concrete thinkers who want facts, and they want them in a straightforward manner. If they perceive you're uncertain or trying to "snow" them, either they'll become more assertive and confrontational or they'll tune you out. Before you give a *Mover & Shaker* their next performance review, reread this section and take it to heart.

Interacting with Narrators

Managing *Narrators* is like directing a stage play. You want to bring out their potential to produce an award-winning performance. At the same time, you don't want them changing the script, behaving like prima donnas, or upstaging one another or you.

Clearly spell out the performance expectations you have for them. Watch that they don't get off track and "do their own thing." The "thing" is an aspect of the job they prefer because in their view it's more fun. But it may not be consistent with your priorities.

On occasion, you may have to rein them in. Do it in a manner that appeals to a *Narrator*, like this: "Maria, I like the enthusiasm you're showing on the Smith account. I'd be thrilled to see you give even more gusto to the Jones account, which, as you know, is our top priority." To a *Narrator* the word "like" sounds like a little clapping. Words like "thrilled," "so pleased,"

"delighted," and "Wow!" roar in their ears like a standing ova-
tion. That's what they want so they'll do what it takes to get it.

Considering your many management responsibilities, it's
easy to neglect *Narrators*. You may be preoccupied with
employees whose performance is marginal or giving attention
to getting problems solved. Besides, these folks appear to be
sufficiently self-motivated.

Watch that you don't ignore *Narrators* or overlook their
efforts. If you do, they may slip into the role of "marginal per-
former" just to get attention from you. Or they may take their
energy and enthusiasm elsewhere. By all means, don't say or
do anything that a *Narrator* might perceive as a put-down.

If you tend toward a highly assertive, even aggressive communication style, take care to curb the inclination to interrupt.
It's tempting when you're talking with a talkative person. If the
Narrator becomes too talkative or takes off on a tangent, interject and redirect them to the topic at hand. When they pause to
breathe, jump in and say something like "I sense you're really
interested in that idea (*this validates them*). Before we talk
about it, though, let's finish up with X (*redirects*)."

If your communication style is more mild-mannered, tending
toward the passive, step it up when interacting with a *Narrator*.
If they don't get expressive responses from you, they'll perceive
you're disinterested in them. That's demotivating. Like an actor
or actress, a *Narrator* feels rejuvenated or rejected depending on
how the audience responds.

Interacting with Care Givers

If you're a task-focused concrete thinker and a person of few
words, the *Care Giver* employees you manage represent "a
challenge and an opportunity" to stretch your communication
skills. Because they value relationships, they'll want to engage
in friendly conversations. Sometimes, they tell you more than
you need or want to know.

You might consider it a waste of time when someone stops
you in the hallway to chat; to a *Care Giver* it means they like you.
You might find office gossip disturbing; to some *Care Givers* it's

Little Things Mean a Lot

TRICKS OF THE TRADE With *Narrators* even small gestures of appreciation go a long way. When they produce a result that warrants recognition, try these ideas—and some of your own creative ones.

- On occasion, leave a voice-mail message that says something as brief and basic as "Good job on your presentation at the meeting." Make this the only message. If you combine it with other business, they'll see it as an afterthought.
- Keep a supply of motivational note cards on hand. Jot down a hand-written note and leave it in their message or incoming box. (*Narrators* love spontaneous gestures.)
- For telecommuters, have balloons delivered to their home-based office.

social networking. You might think using company time for personal phone calls is a violation of policy; to some *Care Givers* it's their way of staying in touch with family and friends. And if they pop in unannounced to talk, to them it's not an untimely interruption. They think they have a good working relationship with the boss (which, by the way, they mean as a compliment to you).

If their sociable behavior exceeds what's appropriate in the work place or preferable to you, point it out as you would with any employee. But bear in mind: many *Care Givers* are sensitive souls who tend to take things personally. Refrain from coming across as insensitive or abrupt. Address them in *Care Giver*-friendly fashion, appealing to their desire to please.

Speak in a kindly, gracious manner. Word corrections like this: "I hope I can *count on you* to make personal phone calls only during your lunch hour or breaks and not on company time." "You'd be *doing me a big favor* by writing out your concern first, and then we'll schedule a time to talk about it." "It *would please me* if you'd let me know the status of your workload before you take on too much."

Say it with a smile. To a *Care Giver* a solemn demeanor suggests you don't like them. And a serious tone of voice sounds like scolding. If you want to get good results from a *Care Giver*, always appear amiable when dealing with them.

If you're a *Narrator* or a *Care Giver* yourself, you should also curb your inclination to talk. Don't monopolize the conversation; hear them out first. Don't join in a conversation with any hint of gossip. Steer conversations back to business, if need be.

Whatever your profile is, with *Care Givers* pick up on highlights of their life. Stop to congratulate them

Draw the Line

As a reflection of their relational nature, some *Care Givers* are only too happy to share personal matters with you. While you want to show interest or express empathy, take care that your behavior can't be misinterpreted as intruding on or getting involved with an employee's personal life. Adhere to the proven principles, "Better safe than sorry" and "Discretion is the greater part of valor."

on their anniversary, the birth of their baby or grandchild. Notice the newest photo on their desk. Thank them for setting up the refreshments for the meeting. And on occasion, give them a compliment.

Interacting with Map Makers

You'll be most effective managing *Map Makers* if, when dealing with them, you role-play a *Map Maker* yourself. As best you can, adopt their communication style and thought pattern.

Give *Map Makers* lead time. Don't drop last-minute "surprises" on them and remark in a cavalier way, "I needed this yesterday." They'll take that as a lack of regard for what they pride themselves on—ensuring that things are done right.

Refrain from giving *Map Makers* the impression you're rushing them, even when that's what you need to do. It's not what you say; it's all in how you put it.

You: The client wants to see a schematic this afternoon.

They: *This afternoon!* (In their mind, they picture the final product and think, "You're crazy!")

You: I know we're only on the first stage of this project. At this point, all we need to show the client is a rough sketch. I know this is unexpected. For that reason, I don't expect the kind of detail you're usually careful to include. What can you put together under the circumstances?

"I know" statements express facts, which *Map Makers* relate to. Reference to "reason," "detail," and "care" appeal to a *Map Maker's* mindset. You're not wasting their time with unrelated information and you're using short sentences in a straightforward manner, which they prefer. You're also giving them permission to be less than absolutely accurate.

They: I don't know .... (They hesitate.) This doesn't give me much time ....

You: I understand. What if we label the schematic "Phase I: Preliminary Plan"? We'll add a footnote that it's subject to change. We'll make it clear to the client that there's still more work to be done before the final plans are ready for their review. (You know the client knows that, but you're giving the *Map Maker* reassurance.) How does that sound?

They: I've got to tell you, I'm not happy about this.

You: Neither am I. I wish the client had given us more notice. With the time you have before 3:00 this afternoon, what can you do?

They: I can give you a rough sketch, but that's all.

A *Map Maker* may still feel rushed, but they'll perceive that you were reasonable in your request.

When you present material to a *Map Maker*, present it as they would—in writing. Substantiate the points you make with evidence in the form of facts and figures. Include charts, graphs, tables, diagrams, or spreadsheets.

When you need to discuss something with a *Map Maker*, if possible make an appointment first. Yes, even when you're the boss and even if it's for only 10 minutes an hour from now. *Map Makers* prefer to be well-prepared. Unlike *Narrators*, spontaneous doesn't suit them. So let them know the time you'd like to see them, specify how much time it'll take, and briefly relate what it's about. Better yet, put it in writing in an e-mail or a note you drop on their desk.

When you recognize *Map Makers* for good performance, emphasize the qualities they value: precision, an excellent solution to the problem, meeting or exceeding the specifications, producing a flawless design.

Manipulation or Management Skill?

Smart
Managing

I've been asked the question, "Don't you think this customizing amounts to manipulation?" The answer: it depends. It depends on your motivation. If your sole motivation is to serve your own interests, then yes, it may be perceived as manipulative. But as a manager, you're concerned with far more than your own interests.

When you're motivated by what's in the best interests of the employee and in the best interests of the organization, no, it's not manipulation. When you use techniques to build better working relationships, it's not manipulation. It's skillful communication and a hallmark of savvy and successful managers.

When in Doubt, Ask

Few people fit neatly into any one tidy profile. Some people have multifaceted personalities. Like a chameleon, they're adaptable by nature and project different personae in differing situations. Others behave differently depending on their mood.

What if you're uncertain about a person's communication profile? Consider the combination of characteristics they display in most situations most of the time. Observe them when they're under pressure. (Often, we show our "true" selves when we're stressed.) Watch and listen closely to how they communicate. Tune in to what they talk about, not only when they talk with you, but also when they talk with their peers.

If you sense you're not reading someone right and you think you could be more effective in your dealings with them, ask what they'd prefer.

- First, check your perception or state your intention.
- Then, ask their preference.

It sounds like this. "I have the impression I'm not stating this clearly. What do you need to hear from me?" Or "I want to recognize the outstanding job you did on the TechnoDot project. I'm thinking of a day off with pay, which would give you time to spend with your family. How does that sound to you?" (This, of course, would appeal to a *Care Giver.*)

The fact that you ask employees for their input will make a favorable impression on them. As a result, they'll be more

Additional Applications

Smart Managing   Although we've concentrated on profiles to understand why and how to customize our communications, the insights they offer can be applied to other things you do.

• *Delegating.* Which employee is best suited to do this task?

• *Motivating.* What's the best way to motivate this employee?

• *Recognizing employees.* Considering this employee's profile, what form of recognition would most appeal to them?

• *Hiring and job placement.* What kind of profile does this job call for? Is this not only a job the person can do, but one they'll like doing so they'll give it their all?

inclined to hold you in higher regard. Not only does that make your interactions with employees more pleasant, it also makes them more productive, which makes you more effective.

The Communicator's Checklist for Chapter 3

❏ The reasonable communication style is expressive (also referred to as assertive), as opposed to the extremes of aggressive, passive, or passive-aggressive styles.

❏ People tend to think according to a predominant thought pattern, either concrete or conceptual.

❏ Communication profiles highlight the primary characteristics of how someone interacts with others. A combination of communication style and thought pattern, the profiles describe *Movers & Shakers*, *Narrators*, *Care Givers*, and *Map Makers*.

❏ You'll be more effective in your interactions with others when you customize your communications to their profiles and preferences.

Building Blocks of Effective Interactions

When they made him an offer he couldn't refuse, Tom accepted a management position with a different company. His first week on the job, he called the employees together for a meeting. He opened on a high note, enthusiastically stating, "I'm confident we can make this the best department in the company." Favoring a contemporary approach to management that welcomes employee input, Tom continued, "I'd like to hear your ideas on how we can do that. What do you think?"

The employees sat in stony-faced silence. Some stared at their shoes. Others doodled on tablets. With vacant expressions, a few looked right past Tom at the wall behind him. One employee took out a cell phone to make a call. No one responded to Tom's question.

He tried again. "You're the troops who work in the trenches. Some of you have been around for awhile. You have a lot of experience on this job and I'd like to hear your ideas for improvement."

After a long and uncomfortable pause, someone from the back of the room spoke up. "Here's an idea. How about we end this meeting and get back to work?" Snickering rippled through the room.

Tom had expected that the time he'd scheduled for the meeting would be filled with a lively exchange of ideas. He hadn't planned any other items for the agenda. Wanting to appear good-natured, he smiled and said, "I have the impression most of you agree?" Still no response. In a last-ditch effort to save face, Tom said, "Let's do that, then. But I'd like you to think about this and we'll meet again next week to discuss your ideas."

Heading back to his office, Tom thought, "What's *wrong* with these people? When I was offered this position, I was told this was a good group. But they sat there like a bunch of deadheads."

Meanwhile, walking back to their work areas, several employees remarked about the meeting. "Yeah, like I'm going to offer any ideas. You remember when I did during a meeting with our last manager? Right in front of everybody she said, 'That's a stupid idea.' See if I ever speak up again."

"What I'd like to know is what he meant by 'ideas for improvement.' I think we're doing a good job. What business does he have telling us we're not the best department? He hasn't been around here long enough to know."

"Well, we're not going to be the best department if he keeps taking up our time in meetings. What are we s'posed to do for the meeting next week?"

"Personally, I don't care. I didn't like his condescending attitude, the way he said we have experience. Of course we do. What does he think we are, a bunch of deadheads?"

What It Means to Be Effective

For more than 50 years, Peter Drucker has been a consultant, teacher, and prolific writer. Highly regarded as "the father of modern management," Drucker defined effectiveness as "doing the right things."

So far, we've considered a few of the "right things" to do when you interact with people, namely:

• Apply the ABC's of constructive communication.

- Manage perceptions, theirs and yours.
- Customize your communication to the profile of the person you're dealing with.

In this chapter, we'll examine additional "right things" to do. To be an effective communicator and an effective manager, they're essential.

Build Rapport

With only a few days on the job, Tom hadn't yet established rapport with the employees. They don't know him well enough to know what his expectations are or if they're "safe" with him. (Can he be trusted? Or, like his predecessor, will he call them "stupid" if he doesn't like their ideas?)

Understandably, they think he doesn't know them well enough to judge their performance. One employee perceived that's exactly what Tom did when he asked for ideas for improvement.

Tom felt it was a fair question. Before he'd accepted the management position, he'd reviewed

> **Rapport** A sense of being connected, in harmony with someone. Rapport facilitates communication. With it, people feel at ease with one another. They're more inclined to speak up and enjoy amiable interactions. Without rapport, we're reluctant to disclose our thoughts. We're more likely to focus on our differences, which can lead to unnecessary misunderstandings.

reports of the department's data and compared these with data from similar functions. One reason he'd taken the job was because he thought he could make some positive changes. The department ranked just average in most categories: productivity, quality control, safety, and customer satisfaction.

But data alone doesn't tell the whole story. It doesn't take into account human factors, like the environment employees worked in under Tom's predecessor. It doesn't reveal the nature of interactions between a manager and employees, the nature of interactions among team members, or the attitudes of individuals in the work group.

Rapport is one of those human factors. And it's one that serves as a motivator. Rapport creates a sense of unity, of belonging. The greater the rapport between you and the employees you rely on for results, the more willing they'll be to go the extra mile for you.

Where differences exist between people, rapport bridges the gap. Simply because of the differences in position, some gap will always exist between a manager and employees. But you can significantly reduce the gap.

How Are You Alike?

In friendly (not formal) conversations, get to know each employee to discover what you have in common. Listen and look for mutual interests, similar experiences, and shared goals. How did the employee get started in the business? What appeals to them about the industry or profession you're both involved in?

You notice a bumper sticker on their car that reads "I'd rather be fishing." You used to go fishing when you were a kid. They do volunteer work in the community. So do you. They have a family photo on their desk. You have a child about the same age as one of theirs. You overhear them talking with excitement about how their favorite sports team won. You're a fan, too. Build on those kinds of commonalities.

Expand Your Horizons

Some people are predisposed to talk about one thing: *their* expertise, *their* investment portfolio, what *they* did over the weekend, the pressures and pleasures of *their* lives. To build rapport with people, expand your conversational style to be inclusive—of others.

How to Win Friends and Influence People has long been regarded a classic on interpersonal skills. In it, Dale Carnegie pointed out that the best conversationalist is not someone who talks well. It's a person who shows interest in what other people like to talk about.

To be better prepared to initiate or join in conversations on various topics, stay abreast of current events. Read the local newspaper. Of course, refrain from controversy. When you join in a conversation, don't take sides on potentially sensitive or explosive issues.

Connecting Through Touch

Studies have shown that touch is a very bonding gesture. It's a visual cue that affirms a person. In an increasingly impersonal world, the personal touch is often lacking in interactions. As such, touch builds rapport. As you know, it's also subject to misinterpretation, especially if the receiver perceives a touch is too personal.

> ### Rapport with the Boss
> Is your boss a reader? If so, notice the books and publications your boss keeps around or talks about, especially those that pertain to business and management. What a person reads is a clue to their interests. Read the same things. When you do, you'll have common points of reference to discuss with your boss. And you'll show yourself to be a person receptive to learning and professional growth.

Some people are natural handshakers and huggers. Others prefer not to be touched at all. If you hug a hugger, others may perceive you're playing favorites. On the other hand, if you don't touch at all, people may perceive you're aloof. So what do you do?

Touch only when the occasion calls for it. And then, touch briefly and appropriately. When you recognize an employee, for example, you might (if

> ### If You Like to Touch, Take Care
> *Never* touch a person inappropriately or in a suggestive manner. Always observe the policy or norms of your organization regarding touch.

you know the employee won't be offended by it) touch their shoulder or arm as you say, "You did a really good job solving that customer's problem." If an employee is visibly upset, you might touch in the same manner to show your concern and reassure them as you say, "Let me know if there's anything I can do to help."

If you're wary of touching (which many managers are nowadays), simply gesture as though you're going to touch without actually touching. The gesture has the effect of closing the gap of space that physically separates people. But stopping short of actually touching removes the risk of giving offense.

Gain Respect

After his aborted meeting, a manager from another department stopped by Tom's office. "How'd your meeting go?" she asked. Tom told her about it, describing how one employee pulled out a cell phone to make a call and others snickered. She remarked, "It's a shame the employees don't respect your authority."

Often, employees don't. In "old order" organizations of the past, employees might have shown respect for a manager simply because they'd been raised to "respect your elders." Nowadays, that's not often the case.

In contemporary organizations, it's also common to find managers who are younger than the employees they manage. Managers aren't always "elders" anymore. In addition, events in recent years have caused many people to distrust authority.

You don't automatically get respect by reason of being a manager. You need to gain it. Why bother? Because people are more inclined to follow the leadership of someone they respect. They're less likely to question you and less likely to stir up trouble.

To gain respect, incorporate in your interactions these three C's:

- Credibility
- Composure
- Constructive comments

Credibility

If you were to ask employees to rank your credibility on a scale of 1 to 10 (with 10 being high), what kind of score would they give you? If you want to be well-respected, aim for a score good enough for a gold medal.

The measure of your credibility is the extent to which employees (and your boss and colleagues) believe what you tell them. Can they rely on your word? Are you trustworthy?

Credibility builds over time, one interaction after another. To establish and maintain your credibility:

- Don't make promises you can't keep. "I promise you'll get the next promotion." "The company's going public next year and you'll all be millionaires." "We've submitted a grant proposal and as soon as we get the funding, you'll get a big raise." Promises like these raise hopes and you don't want to be the one to dash people's hopes. If you made a promise and later find you can't keep it because conditions have changed, let the person know right away. Give them an honest explanation of the reason you can't keep the promise you made.
- Do what you say you'll do. If an employee brings a matter to you and you say, "I'll get back to you on this," do so—promptly.
- Keep employees informed. In "old order" organizations, secrecy was (and in some cases still is) customary. Managers with a better understanding of human nature take an enlightened view. They recognize that an atmosphere of secrecy breeds suspicion and undermines people's ability to coordinate their work in ways that lead to higher productivity. Secrecy also undermines trust in the organization and damages management's credibility. Many contemporary managers now appreciate that if it affects employees, let them know about it. And if employees can make a contribution, include them in "the loop."

  "Old order" organizations often consider information about budgets and financial performance proprietary to managers. In the best contemporary organizations, not only is such information shared with employees, but they're the ones who develop the budget for their team and they assume accountability for the team's performance as a profit and loss center.
- Be the first they hear news from, both good and bad. It's tough to be the bearer of bad news, but sometimes it falls

on you to report what people would rather not hear. It's better they hear it from you than through the rumor mill, where facts get distorted and blown out of proportion.

- Make your motto, "No bluff, no guff." People don't expect you to know everything. They just want you to be straight with them.

If you're asked a question you don't know the answer to, respond with the most applicable option. You might refer the matter back to the person who asked: "That's a good question. Why don't you research it and let me know what you come up with?" Refer it to someone else who has expertise in the area: "Check with Paul in Human Resources. He'll know how the policy applies in your situation." Or offer to look into the matter yourself and let them know when you'll get back to them with an answer. (Notice this is the last option. If you do this all of the time, you'll spend more time looking into matters than you will managing.)

Your credibility is also determined not only by what you say, but by how you conduct yourself. Remember the old adage, "Actions speak louder than words." The greatest credibility enhancer there is is to deliver on your promises.

Tricks of the Trade

On the Spot?

Are you ever caught off guard, not fully prepared with a sterling response on the tip of your tongue? You're in a managers' meeting and one of your colleagues has just finished a presentation. The boss turns to you and asks, "What's your opinion about this?" Or an employee meets with you to discuss their idea for improving operations. They ask, "What do you think?"

When you're put on the spot—asked what you think when you haven't had time to think or to formulate a credible response—buy time. Say something like "Terry presented some good points. I'd like to crunch the numbers before I come to a conclusion" or "I think it's an important issue and I'd like to give it more thought."

By buying time, you don't blurt out a hasty opinion you may live to regret. In most cases, people will respect you for taking the time to carefully consider issues and ideas. That adds to your credibility.

Composure

Remaining composed, especially under pressure, is a mark of maturity. And if there's one thing employees (and bosses) expect from managers, it's maturity. Composure is also (as you may recall from Chapter 1) a mark of self-confidence.

Is there an employee you manage whose conduct "rattles your cage," so to speak? Do you ever interact with someone whose communication behaviors push your "hot buttons" and you see red? If you sense you're close to losing your composure, slow your breathing. Reflect on this question: "When this incident is over, how do I want *my* behavior remembered?"

If the incident is between you and one other person, from your continued composure they'll get the message they can't get to you. If the incident occurs in the presence of others, everyone who witnesses it will be favorably impressed that you remained calm and composed. And they'll respect you for it.

Constructive Comments

In his meeting with employees, Tom made a constructive comment when he said, "I'm confident we can make this the best department in the company." At the time, it didn't have the positive effect he intended. But a month or so later, after he established rapport and gained the employees' respect, the same statement might be greeted with applause and a rousing chorus of "You bet!"

Constructive comments:

- express enthusiasm
- communicate positive expectations
- offer reassurance
- affirm your belief in the individual or in the team
- convey conviction that together you can recover from a setback, overcome the obstacle, resolve this conflict, and come out ahead.

As a manager, you're in a leadership role. Employees take their cues from you. They may bad-mouth the business, criticize the management, carp about pay or working conditions, complain about customers—because sometimes that's what some employees do. But they don't like hearing complaints and criticisms from you. Respect is paid to the person who holds themselves to a higher standard of conduct and communication.

If you can't find something constructive to say, don't say anything at all.

And of course, don't let your boss overhear you making critical or complaining remarks. Just as you want the employees you manage to propose solutions, rather than constantly coming to you with problems, that's what your boss wants from you, too.

OK, you've established rapport. You've gained the respect of your boss, colleagues, and the employees you manage. What next?

Gear to the Level of Readiness

In his meeting, Tom was disappointed that none of the employees responded when he asked about ideas for improvement. We've addressed some of the reasons they may have been reluctant to speak up. Here's another. Maybe no one in the group had ideas or the confidence to express them.

Gear your communications to the level of the employees you manage. Think of it this way. If you're driving along an open stretch of highway with little traffic and good weather conditions, you can shift your car into high gear and move ahead at high speed. Conversely, if you're driving in stormy weather on downtown streets where traffic is congested, you shift down to a lower gear and drive at slower speeds (or you should). In other words, you consider the conditions and adjust accordingly. Do the same when you interact with employees.

> **Key Term**
> **Low readiness** or **high readiness** The degree to which an employee or a team is ready to participate in planning, problem solving, decision making, and innovation.

Low-Readiness Employees/Work Groups

These are novices or rookies. They're still in a learning mode: acquiring skills, becoming familiar with the business, and gaining confidence. When a problem occurs, often they don't know what to do to solve it; they need help. They're manager-dependent.

When you manage low-readiness employees, shift into low gear. Apply the following guidelines.

- Communicate frequently. Provide ongoing guidance and lots of reassurance.
- Communicate more formally, often in writing. Be explicit.
- Delegate tasks, giving detailed instructions. Describe precisely what you need done and spell out specifically how to do it. Require your approval before final action. Use delegation as a form of employee development.
- Set up times at frequent intervals for employees to report to you so you can closely monitor results and offer correction or recognition.

High-Readiness Employees/Teams

These are veterans: highly skilled, highly familiar with the business, highly reliable when working on their own. Typically, they anticipate potential problems because they've been around long enough or know the operation well enough to spot when something's amiss. They take the initiative to resolve the situation. We refer to them as self-motivated, self-supervising employees and self-directed or self-managed teams.

From training, experience, and coaching, they're able to function at a high level of independence. By delegation and access to information, they've been empowered to make decisions and implement action. Management serves primarily in an oversight role.

When you manage high-readiness employees, you can speed things up. Apply the following guidelines.

- Communicate on an as-needed basis. Redirect their efforts when necessary. Ask for their input. Provide motivation.
- Communicate informally; often a brief chat will suffice. Give overviews and summaries.
- Delegate projects. Describe *what* you want: the outcome or objectives to be achieved. Leave it up to the

highly experienced employee or self-directed team to determine *how* to produce the result. Give them the authority to take action and then apprise you of what they've done.

- Periodically check on progress. Ask to be briefed on potential problems in case you need to intervene.

Intent and Interpretation

During the meeting with employees, Tom said, "You have a lot of experience." He meant the remark in a positive way, as a compliment that affirmed their abilities. At least one employee took it negatively, perceiving that Tom was being condescending.

Does that ever happen to you? Your intent is misinterpreted. Do you sometimes misinterpret what other people intend? A breakdown in communication can occur if you don't clearly express your intent or if the other person misinterprets it.

Here's where much of what we've discussed so far comes into play. Your intent is more likely to be misinterpreted when one or a combination of these factors exist:

- an atmosphere of secrecy, rather than open communication.
- a lack of rapport.
- a lack of information or experience: a supervisor new to the job should avoid comments that extend beyond what they know.
- little commonality: people don't share a similar frame of reference and mutual understandings of goals, objectives, and expectations.
- inconsistencies in the verbal, vocal, and visual cues you convey.
- disruptions that distract people and interfere with a clear reception of your message.
- a lack of clarity in your communication: meanings get muddled if, when you speak or write, you use jargon, polysyllabic terminology, sarcasm, veiled hints, numerous or unnecessary details, digressions, and/or long-winded

and run-on sen-
tences like this one.

Getting Your Message Across as You Mean It

To improve the probability
that your communications
are interpreted as you
intend, follow these steps.

Clarity Is Key

The purpose of communica-
tion is to express, not
impress. The more important the message, the more critical it is to lessen the
likelihood of misinterpretation. Consider: what is the *clearest* and most *con-
cise* way to express what I have to say?

The most effective communicators
apply the familiar formula KISS: Keep
It Short and Simple.

1. Before you communi-
   cate (speak or write),
   have clearly in mind the outcome you want. When the communication is critical (such as performance reviews, assign-
   ing priorities, delegating, giving a presentation, reporting to
   your boss), write out your objective ahead of time. What do
   you want to happen as a result of what you say?
2. Begin with something that sparks the interest of your listeners or readers. What will capture their attention? What will
   prompt them to set aside whatever else they're thinking
   about or doing so they give you their undivided attention?
3. State your message in a manner that speaks to them: their
   frame of reference, profile, and level. When communicating
   to a diverse group, talk in terms that address the greatest
   number of people in the group. For main points you don't
   want anyone to miss, start with a broad statement, then
   clarify it with an example or more detailed explanation.
4. To check the listeners' understanding, before going on to
   the next point, invite questions. Say, "I want to be sure I've
   been clear. What questions do you have?" Look like you
   expect questions. Pause to give people time to formulate
   their thoughts.
5. Express your message clearly. If necessary, to shed light on
   what you mean, use a comparison, metaphor, analogy,
   story, or graphic illustration. But don't overdo it.
6. Stick to the point. Don't ramble. Don't digress. And don't
   let others sidetrack you.

Well-Meant Intent

TRICKS OF THE TRADE Imagine if everyone had radar imbedded in their brain. If this internal radar picks up a signal of a potential threat, an alarm sounds. To protect themselves from attack (even the perception of a possible verbal attack), people tend to tune out and shut down. Or they prepare to counterattack. From that point on, they hear very little of what you say.

To prompt people to listen up and to predispose them to favorably interpret your communication, start with a statement of well-meant intent. Well-meant intent conveys a positive point. When a person's "radar" receives it, they think, "I want to hear this."

For example, you could say, "You made mistakes on this report. (The listener's alarm goes off.) We can't send it out this way." Some employees would interpret that you're telling them, "The report's a mess and it's your fault."

A statement of well-meant intent would sound like this: "Overall, I'm pleased with the way you put this report together. Before it goes out in final, I need you to correct a few errors." Interpretation: you did a good job; let's make it even better.

7. Recap and wrap. Briefly restate the main point(s) of your message. Why? Because not everyone listens closely or catches your meaning the first time.

To Minimize Misinterpretations

Even when communication is clear, it's still subject to misinterpretation. One misunderstanding can breed further misunderstandings. That can lead to unnecessary tension, even resentment. Clear the air.

- **Correct misinterpretations.** If you're aware you've been misunderstood, state what you did *not* mean, followed by what you *do* mean. Take Tom's remark, "You have a lot of experience." Suppose the employee who was offended by it said to Tom, "You don't need to patronize us." To correct the misinterpretation, Tom would say, "I did *not* mean to sound patronizing. I meant the remark as a compliment."
- **Clarify their intent.** If you're uncertain how to interpret what someone says, don't assume the worst. When in

doubt, find out. Ask. Restate verbatim what the other person said. Then ask, "What did you mean by that?" or "How do you intend me to take that?" Say it calmly, with composure. Make focused eye contact and speak in a neutral tone of voice.

Here's how it sounds. An employee comes to you and complains about the extra work they've had to do since another employee quit last month. You explain that you're recruiting to fill the vacancy. You ask them to be patient a while longer. They say, "That's just the kind of thing managers always say." Respond in a matter-of-fact manner. "I heard you say, 'That's just the kind of thing managers always say.' What do you mean?"

Clarifying intent may seem similar to perception checking (discussed in Chapter 2). Notice the difference. Perception checking would sound like this: "From your comment, I have the impression you're not satisfied with what I said." It relates a perception you've formed and is based largely on feelings. Clarifying intent restates exactly what the other person said and focuses on getting at the facts of the content. And it holds a person accountable for what they say.

Effective Interactions Take ALL Skills

Three skills are the cornerstones of constructive communication:

- Ask
- Look
- Listen

The acronym ALL makes them easy to remember.

A: Ask

There are basically three types of questions.

1. **Definitive.** These questions define the respondent's position or a situation with a simple "Yes" or "No." Are you finished with the report? Will you present this topic at the meeting? Can we improve customer service? Do you like your job?

You get the quickest answer when you ask a definitive question. But you also get the least amount of information and often little or no explanation.

2. **Directional**. Phrased with the word "which," the answer to this type of question lets you know the direction in which a person wants to go, out of a certain number of options. For example, "For the meeting, I need someone to present Topic A and someone to present Topic B. Which would you prefer?"

   You can point a person in the direction you want them to go by phrasing the question "If ... would ...." Here's how that sounds: "Topic A will take more time to prepare. If I get someone to help you out, would you be willing to present it?"

3. **Open-ended questions**. Called "open" because there are no restrictions on the answers, these questions engage people in dialogue. They're the most effective to ask when you need information or want an explanation.

   Open-ended questions begin with *Who, What, When, Where,* and *How*. Here's how they sound, compared with definitive questions—which usually require a yes or no response, perhaps with explanation.

   • When will you be finished with the report? (vs. Are you finished with the report?)
   • Who'd like to present this topic? (vs. Will you present this topic?)
   • What can we do to improve productivity? (vs. Can we improve productivity?)
   • What do you like about your job? (vs. Do you like your job?)

Notice how the open-ended form of question sounds less abrupt. In some situations, it also conveys a greater interest on your part in the person you're talking to. If someone seems reluctant to speak up, often you can draw them out by asking a well-phrased open question or two. After asking, pause to indicate your willingness to wait for a response. If you're not getting a response from those of whom you've asked an open-ended question, find out if they understand the question or

what else might be caus-
ing the reluctance to
answer.

L: Look

People say a great deal
even when they're not talking. How? By their visual
cues. You can learn a lot—
if you're looking.

Chapter 3 suggested
you can pick up clues to a
person's profile by observ-
ing items in their surroundings. When you interact
with someone, observe the
person, too. When you're

> ### Why Not Why?
> **Smart Managing**
>
> Refrain from asking
> "Why?"—especially if you're
> talking with someone who tends to
> react defensively. Some people take
> *Why* questions personally; they feel
> they're being tested or put on the
> spot. Ask a *Why* question and you set
> yourself up for an answer like "Why
> not?" or "I don't know."
>
> When you want to know why,
> phrase the question using *What* or
> *How*. For example, instead of asking,
> "Why did you do it that way?" ask,
> "What were your reasons for doing it
> that way?" or "How did you decide
> on that approach?"

talking, watch for the nonverbal feedback they express through
facial expressions, gestures, and body movements.

Suppose someone raises an eyebrow. It's a signal: of a
question? skepticism? disagreement? If you're not observant,
you won't notice the visual cue. If you do notice it, you won't
know what it means unless you clarify their intent. Once you've
done that, you can respond accordingly.

In some situations, managers who feel uneasy look down or
away from the person they're talking to. I've observed managers who, while giving performance reviews that were bad
news, read from the form on their desk. If you asked them,
"How did the employee react?" they couldn't tell you—because
they weren't looking.

Be sensitive to the moment. If you approach an employee's
desk and the individual is visibly preoccupied with a task, it's
not the best time to give corrective feedback. If you notice he or
she is talking on the phone, wait before giving instructions.
These points might have been prefaced with the phrase, "It goes
without saying ..." Except it doesn't.

In the quick and quickening pace many of us keep up these

What Do You See?

A *Fortune* 100 company included in its sales training program an exercise in observation. The reps in training made simulated sales calls on an instructor who played the role of a customer. Afterwards, the reps were asked to list everything they'd observed, from objects in the office to the customer's reactions.

Later in their careers, some of those reps became the best managers. They transferred their finely honed skills of observation from dealing with customers to dealing with employees. Because these managers had learned to observe, they were keenly aware of the visual cues employees conveyed.

days, sometimes we overlook the obvious. Preoccupied with our own "to dos" and in a rush to get them done, it's easy to become oblivious to what others are doing. Slow down and look around.

L: Listen

On the lines below, list things people do that indicate they are *not* listening to you. (If you need more space, use a separate sheet of paper or write in the margins.)

Now, read over your list and place a checkmark next to those things you sometimes do when employees (or your boss or colleagues) talk to you.

When you sense a person you're talking to isn't listening to you, how do you feel? Fill in the blank: _____ _____. Is that how you want employees to feel? (Is that how you want your boss to feel?)

> **Attentive listening** Giving undivided attention to the person who's speaking. It's especially important to listen attentively when you're engaged in a significant interaction: a problem-solving discussion, a performance review, a conversation with an employee or your boss about a matter of concern to them. If, while they're talking, you turn your attention to something else (answer the phone, check your pager, flip through files, scan your e-mail), the message you send that person is "This other thing I'm doing is more important than you are." Attentive listening is also sometimes called "active listening."

Key Term

Of all the interpersonal communication skills, listening is one of the most important. It signifies we're "connecting" with the person speaking. That's essentially what constructive communication is all about: making connections that contribute to building bridges of productive relationships. When you don't listen, you lose an opportunity to do that. To listen attentively:

- Make focused and meaningful eye contact. Look at the person, not at things around you.
- Give appropriate feedback: nod your head when you agree, occasionally utter, "Uh-huh."
- Don't interrupt. Often, people work up to the most important point and express it last. If you interrupt before they've finished speaking, you may miss what's really on their mind.
- Don't finish people's sentences for them.
- As much as possible, eliminate external distractions like ringing telephones and interruptions from others.
- Eliminate "internal noise"—thoughts that buzz though your brain and interfere with hearing what someone's saying.
- While someone is speaking, refrain from making assumptions or judgments. (It may show in your facial expression and send them a negative visual cue.) Don't formulate how you're going to respond. If you second-guess them, you may get it wrong.
- Paraphrase when appropriate. It sounds like this: "If I understand your question correctly, you want to know how we're going to implement this change. Is that right?" Briefly restate

what you heard (a) to confirm that you're accurately inter-
preting their intended meaning, (b) to indicate you're listening, or (c) to buy time to formulate your response.

- Think about how you'd paraphrase what they're saying.
  Even if you don't actually do it, thinking about it keeps
  you focused on listening because you can't paraphrase if
  you haven't heard what they've said.
- When a person has finished speaking, before you get into
  what you have to say, offer a validating statement that
  reflects on what they've said. It confirms you were listening. Even if you don't agree with the point they made, it
  validates a person when you say something like "I can
  understand your concern," "I can tell you're enthused
  about this," "Thank you for bringing it to my attention," or
  "That's one way of looking at this issue."

What if someone comes to talk to you at an inconvenient
time, when you can't give them your undivided attention? First
ask, "What is this about?" Their answer helps you determine
whether the matter is something they consider crucial and
they'll want your full attention. If it is, let them know this is not a
good time.

Say something like "Since this is important to you, I want to
give you my complete attention. It's not possible for me to do
that right now. Let's set aside a time to talk about this. How's
4:00 this afternoon?" Schedule the time then and there and for
as soon as possible so they won't feel you're brushing them off.

In Douglas Adams' *The Hitchhiker's Guide to the Galaxy*,
this dialogue occurs between two characters.

Arthur: "It's times like this I wish I'd listened to my mother."
Ford: "Why, what did she say?"
Arthur: "I don't know. I never listened."

A problem erupts. A disgruntled employee quits. A project is
falling behind schedule. The work group is splintered by conflict.
The legal department pays a visit. And the boss asks you,
"What's going on?" Don't put yourself in the position of having to
answer, "I don't know. I never listened." Make listening a priority.

To Reduce Interruptions

You want to listen attentively, but it's not always feasible to do so, especially with interruptions about mundane matters that don't warrant your full attention.

- If you're interrupted with questions about procedures, create written procedures or develop a manual of FAQs (Frequently Asked Questions), either in print or computerized.
- If interruptions are related to a lack of skill, provide training.
- Name an experienced person as "lead" for the work group. Direct employees to take their questions first to the lead person.
- If many interruptions are on matters of a lesser priority that can wait, schedule a routine time of 10 or 15 minutes once or twice a day to cover such matters with employees at one sitting.
- Mount an in-box on the wall *outside* your office or cubicle. Ask employees to place notes of "can-wait" items there. Respond to their queries daily.
- If an employee persists in interrupting you unnecessarily, give them corrective feedback.
- Don't remain cloistered behind closed doors all day. If you do, some employees will interrupt just to get your attention. Schedule times during the day or week when you're visible and available to employees in their work areas.

The Communicator's Checklist for Chapter 4

❏ Build rapport and gain respect.

❏ Consistently convey credibility, composure, and keep your comments constructive.

❏ Follow the steps to clearly communicate the meaning you intend, beginning with well-meant intent. Minimize misinterpretations.

❏ Use ALL your skills. Ask open questions. Look to pick up on visual cues. Listen attentively.

Communicating So They Get It Right

You want results. But you don't want just any old results. You don't want results that need to be reworked. You don't want results that fall short of objectives. You want good results.

Good results lead to achieving the goals of your operation. They contribute to the success of the organization. And they reflect your managerial skill.

Reasons Employees Don't Produce Good Results

When employees don't produce the results you need, usually you can trace it to one of the following reasons.

1. They don't know they're supposed to. This is an issue of performance management.
2. They don't know how to. They lack the skill or haven't received directions. This is related to hiring, training, and giving instructions.
3. They don't want to. They have an indifferent or negative attitude, which is a matter of motivation and correction.
4. They don't have adequate resources: not enough time,

materials, equipment, or supplies. This is a matter of money and resource allocation.

Since we're focusing on effective interactions, we'll consider how to improve results in the first three areas by communicating:

> **Feedback** What you "feed back" to a person in response to something they've done. Without feedback from you, employees don't know for certain how you think they're doing. Feedback is a way of letting employees know you're paying attention to their performance—and doing something about it.

Key Term

- Instructions
- Corrective feedback
- Positive feedback

Giving Instructions

Take a task as simple as making a cheese sandwich. If you were giving me instructions on how to make one, what would you say?

"Take two slices of bread. Add cheese." I already know that. "OK," you say, "then make me the sandwich." When you get it, you're not happy with the result. I made a cheddar cheese sandwich on white bread; you wanted Swiss cheese on rye. I used mayonnaise; you wanted mustard. I sliced it crosswise; you like your sandwiches cut diagonally. Well, I didn't know all of those details.

If you're thinking, "It's no big deal. It's just a sandwich," you're right. But when it comes to the work you get from employees, usually it is a big deal (or at least a bigger deal than a sandwich).

Getting the result you want starts with giving complete and accurate instructions. This occurs in three stages: before you give instructions, when you're giving instructions, and after the task is done.

Before You Give Instructions

Plan what you're going to do. When you formulate your thoughts ahead of time, you're prepared to articulate instructions more clearly and completely. That can help reduce oversights and errors. The time you take at the front end can save time when you meet with the employee to give instructions and when the employee works on the task. And you and the employee will be happier with the result.

So before you give instructions, give thought to the task and what it entails.

- *Is this a one-time task or is it something that will be done repeatedly?* If it's going to recur on a regular basis, can your instructions be prepared as a written procedure? Initially, it may take more time to write a procedure, but in the long run it'll save time and help to reduce errors.
- *Is the task relatively simple and straightforward? Or is it multi-faceted, consisting of several segments?* If the latter, consider giving instructions in stages, separately for each segment. That way, you can offer any needed corrections before beginning the next segment. You can ensure each stage meets requirements and satisfies your expectations before the job gets too far along.
- *Is it a standalone task? Or is it one part of a larger process or project?* If it's the latter, this one task will likely affect others, so accuracy and quality are especially important.
- *What's the final destination?* Will the end result remain in your department? Go to your boss? Be distributed to other departments? Go out to customers or clients? What impression do you want it to make on the person(s) receiving it?
- *Will the end result be reviewed for compliance or accreditation?*
- *Is this task of lesser or greater importance than other things the employee does?* What instruction will you give the employee regarding priorities?

You'll also want to identify beforehand the What, Who, When, Where, How, and Why of the task. These are questions an employee may have in mind when you give instructions.

What. Define the end result and describe critical criteria. The more important the task, the more specific you'll want to be. Write down requirements or specifications that must be met to complete the end result as you need it done.

A written list serves to remind you of all of the bases you want to be sure to cover when you give instructions. Without it, you may inadvertently neglect to mention a point, giving the employee reason to excuse errors or omissions. They'll be right when they say, "You didn't tell me *that*."

Using our previous example, here's how your list might look. End result: cheese sandwich. Details: three slices of Swiss cheese, two slices of rye bread, Dijon mustard on one of the slices of bread, the sandwich to be sliced in half diagonally.

Too much detail? Yes, for people who know how to make a sandwich the way you like it. But not for someone who doesn't know what you want. Imagine if they've never seen a sandwich or never made one for you before. If you say "mustard on one slice," does that mean on a slice of cheese or on a slice of bread? *You* have in mind what you want. But the employee working on the task might not know what you have in mind or their conception may differ from yours.

Who. Determine who would be best suited to do the task. Consider employees' skills, communication profiles, and the level of readiness the task requires. Also make note of who the employee should go to if they have questions or need assistance.

When. This is the date the completed task is due back to *you* (not the date it's due to your boss or a client). Be realistic about time frames and, when possible, build in a buffer of extra time.

Suppose you need a report by the 10th and you figure it'll take two days to prepare. Don't instruct the employee (especially a novice) to complete it by the 10th. Ask to have it done by the 8th (or sooner). That allows for a day in case corrections or changes need to be made. What's the second extra day for? *You* might be able to do the report in two days, but can the employee? They may not be as proficient as you are at the type

How Much Detail?

The degree of detail you communicate when you give instructions will vary, depending on the following factors. Know:

• whether the employee has ever done this or a similar task before.

• what they already know versus what they don't know. Don't waste their time or yours going over things they already know. On the other hand, you don't want to miss telling them something they need to know to give you the result you want.

• how available you'll be to answer questions that may come up while the task is being done. The less available you are, the more detail you'll want to provide at the outset.

of task or their time may be constricted by multiple priorities and frequent interruptions.

If the task or project will be done over a period of time, note when you'll want to meet with the employee for interim follow-up.

Where. Indicate where to find information and materials. If the task requires the use of outside services, instruct the employee where to have such services done.

Why. Think about times past when a manager delegated a job to you. Did you ever feel "dumped on"? When you were given instructions, did you ever think the task was just so much "busy work"? That's what employees sometimes perceive.

When you're planning how to communicate instructions, imagine if the employee were to ask, "So what?" How would you answer the question?

Let employees know why a task is important. Communicate the value in what they'll be doing, the contribution their efforts will make. Typically, when people know why their work matters, they're more motivated to do their best.

How. Describe how to proceed through the task, step by step, from beginning to end.

There's an obvious exception to specifically describing the "how to." It's not necessary when you delegate to a high-readiness employee and you're confident they can produce the result you want on their own initiative. Then, just be sure they're clear about the "What."

The *Worksheet for Communicating Instructions* (Figure 5-1) summarizes the key points to consider when you prepare to give instructions.

Worksheet for Communicating Instructions

What   (end result) _____

For (destination) _____

Criteria _____

_____

Type of task _____   Priority _____

Who   Assigned to _____

When   Date assigned _____ / ____ / _____

Final due date _____ / ____ / _____

Due from employee _____ / ____ / _____

Follow-up date(s) for
progress reports _____ / ____ / _____

_____ / ____ / _____

Where   Sources of information, materials, services _____

_____

Why _____

Figure 5-1.

When You Give Instructions

The preceding chapter pointed out that effective communication begins by knowing the outcome you want. What's your objective when you give instructions? The employee will clearly understand what you want done and they'll be able to do it to your satisfaction. To accomplish your objective of getting a good result, follow the guidelines covered in the previous section and follow these steps.

1. **The Right Time.** What's the right time to give instructions? When the employee is free to give you their full attention and when you can concentrate on explaining what you want. If the employee is preoccupied with something else or frequently interrupted, they may not hear or may forget an important instruction. If you're distracted, you may miss making a point.

2. **The Right Way.** Remember to relate to the employee you're giving instructions to. Adapt your communication to their vocabulary, communication profile, and level of readiness.

3. **Visual Reference.** Whenever possible, provide a tangible example of what you're instructing the employee to do: a sample, diagram, model, rendering, or graphic. If you're giving instructions to set up a spreadsheet, for example, do you have a pencil sketch you can show the employee to illustrate what you have in mind? If you're giving instructions to compile a report, is there a similar report you can refer to that the employee can use as a guide?

4. **Pause for Questions.** When your instructions include several steps, after every few points ask, "What questions do you have?" It gives the employee a chance to ask for clarification if they need it. Just because someone's nodding while you're talking doesn't mean they fully follow what you're saying. It doesn't mean they don't, but you want to be sure.

5. **Ask for a Replay.** When you've finished giving the instructions, do not ask, "Did you get it?" or "Do you understand?" Some people hear tacked on to the end of such questions an

implied "dummy" ("Did you get it, dummy?"). If there's something in the instructions they don't understand, some employees won't speak up because they don't want to risk being thought of as "stupid."

Instead, ask the employee to repeat the instructions back to you. Say something like "I want to be sure I've been clear. So if you'd restate for me, please, what I've asked you to do." Listen closely

How to Ask for Questions

Never ask, "Do you have any questions?" Phrased that way, the listener thinks, "No, does she think I'm stupid?" Or they think, "Yes, but it's probably a dumb question so I'm not going to ask." A question that begins "Do you...?" can be answered "Yes" or "No." Even if "Yes," the employee has a question, often to avoid embarrassment they'll say "No."

Phrase your question with "What." It sounds like you presume there are questions. When you give the impression that you expect questions, people are more likely to ask.

as the employee reviews your instructions to make sure they haven't missed anything.

When you ask the employee to restate your instructions, be sure your tone of voice and facial expression are pleasant. Otherwise, they may get the impression you're quizzing them; they'll feel you're putting them on the spot.

If the due date is crucial, also ask, "And when will you have this done?"

6. **Progress Reports**. Does the task call for interim follow-up? If so, as you finish giving your instructions, say something like "Let's get together this same time next week so you can bring me up to date on the progress you've made." This conveys the positive message that you expect the employee will make progress.

Do not say, "Let's get together so I can see how you're doing." This wording implies that you're going to check up on them, which may be perceived negatively.

Instructions to Novice and Agreeable Types

Be sure to confirm your instructions and set up short-term time frames for follow-up when it's the first time an employee will be doing a task of this type or when you're dealing with an employee who has an agreeable nature.

It may take a novice longer to do a task than it would an experienced employee and it may require closer supervision from you. Employees with an agreeable personality nod agreeably (yes, they understand your instructions) and nod agreeably (yes, they can do it on time) even if they don't or can't. In both cases, avoid the potential problem of not getting the end result when you need it.

Use phrasing like "I count on you to..." or "I trust that you will complete this as we've agreed." Words like *count on* and *trust* imply a sense of obligation.

While you're talking with the employee, ask them to post the follow-up and final due dates on their calendar. Let them see you write the dates in your calendar. These are visual cues that convey you're committed to the dates. Urge them to let you know if they start to slip behind schedule. Don't do this in a manner that implies you're checking up on them. Instead emphasize that it's important to meet deadlines because you and others are depending on them.

After the Task Is Done

You've given the employee instructions. They've carried them out. To complete the cycle of giving instructions:

- Give the employee feedback: positive when the job is done well, corrective if there's room for improvement.
- Assess your effectiveness. If the end result isn't satisfactory, is there some aspect of how you communicated instructions that you can improve the next time around?

Giving Corrective Feedback

Let's listen in on a couple of conversations. The first is between two employees.

Joe: I'm fed up with his constant complaints.

Jane: I know what you mean. It's a real bummer coming to work some days, knowing you've got to put up with his grumbling.

Joe: This morning, I had that report to get out. He must have interrupted me five times for no good reason. And when you try to say something to him, he gets angry, like it's your fault.

Jane: Yeah, and what's with his showing up late all the time? I can't believe what he gets away with around here.

Joe: I don't know why Kim doesn't do something about it."

Jane: Well, you know how managers are.

In an office down the hall, this second conversation is going on between two managers.

Kim: Have you got a few minutes?

Toby: Sure. What's up?

Kim: You've been a manager longer than I have. I could use some advice.

Toby: Personnel problem?

Kim: Yep. How'd you guess?

Toby: That's usually what it is.

Kim: This one's tough. One of the guys in my group has been coming in late most days. He's late showing up for work, late getting back from lunch. The only thing he does early is leave. I'm afraid it's not fair to the others.

Toby: Have you talked to him about it?

Kim: I tried to, but he got defensive.

Toby: How's his attitude about the job?

Kim: Not good. In fact, I think it's starting to affect some of the people he works with. They seem to be avoiding him.

Toby: You know you have to confront the situation.

Kim: I know. But I just hate having to do it. I'm no good at confrontation.

Not knowing what to do or how to do it effectively, or just dreading a difficult and painful encounter, some managers put off confronting a performance problem. You hope it'll go away or take care of itself. It rarely does.

The Drawbacks to Delay

If you don't confront a performance problem to get it corrected, the odds are:

Key Term **Performance problem** A repeated pattern of behavior that has a detrimental effect on the performance of the individual and/or the work group. Often it's called unacceptable or inappropriate behavior. It's the habitual nature of an undesirable behavior that makes it a performance problem.

- **It will continue.** In some cases, an employee may not be aware that what they're doing is a problem so they continue to do it. In other cases, the employee knows the behavior is unacceptable or inappropriate. But as long as they get away with it, they have no reason to change.

- **It will escalate.** When a performance problem is not addressed, often it increases in frequency or intensity.

- **It will spread.** Other employees pick up the message, too. When some employees get away with poor performance or unacceptable or inappropriate behavior, other employees think, "If it's OK for them to do it, it's OK for me to do it, too." If enough employees follow suit, norms of counterproductive behavior form and infect the work group.

- **It lowers morale and productivity.** Other employees bear the brunt of performance problems that are not corrected. They have to pick up the slack or put up with a coworker's undesirable behavior. In time, morale slips. When morale declines, so does productivity. You can't achieve high productivity with low morale. Customer service will be adversely affected, too.

Clearly, the consequences of not confronting a performance problem obstruct your mission as a manager: to produce *desirable* results through the performance of others.

Overcoming Reluctance to Confront

Call to mind a performance problem that occurs with an employee you manage, some behavior you'd like to see the employee correct or improve.

Confront To meet face to face. Formed from the prefix *con,* meaning "with," and derived from the Latin *frons,* meaning *front of the head* or *face,* the original definition of "confront" was "with face." When you think in terms of the origins of the word, you'll find it easier to confront an employee about a performance problem. It's merely a matter of facing up to the issue or dealing directly with it, by discussing it face to face.

"Confront" is not synonymous with "confrontation," which often has negative connotations. Done correctly, there's no reason giving corrective feedback should lead to a confrontation.

In the space below, briefly describe the behavior and its consequences.

Behavior: _____

Consequences of the performance problem:

_____

_____

_____

Describe the behavior you'd prefer. In other words, what do you want the employee to do instead of what they're doing now? Make note of the results of the preferred behavior.

Preferred: _____

Positive results of the preferred behavior:

_____

_____

_____

For yourself, for the group you manage, and for the organization, which would you rather have? Of course, you'd rather get the results of the preferred behavior.

Now, briefly describe how each of the following feels to you.

Confronting the employee: _____

Not confronting the employee: _____

Which feels better? For many of us, not confronting feels better than confronting. When we think about confronting an employee, we picture an unpleasant scene. In our imagination, we magnify how the employee will react. Most of us choose "better" and avoid "worse." Since confronting seems worse, we don't do it.

Let's look at this a different way. You confront the employee about the behavior. The individual corrects it. The situation improves. The employee's coworkers are happier. Better results are produced. How does *that* feel? It feels better than the consequences of unacceptable behavior, especially when you consider that ongoing performance problems reflect on you as a manager.

When you need to deal with a performance problem, compare what it will be like when the matter is resolved with what the problem may do if you don't confront it. To motivate yourself to face up to a performance problem, focus on the prospect of a positive outcome.

As a manager, you're charged with an overriding responsibility: to do what is in the best interests of the business over time. It's always in the best interests of the employee, your team, the organization, and your success as a manager to get counterproductive attitudes and actions corrected.

What About Attitudes?

When a performance problem is related to attitude, managers are sometimes stumped. You may have heard you're not supposed to

---

The Person Is <u>Not</u> the Problem

Smart Managing   Resist the inclination to think of the employee as a problem. It's what the employee does or doesn't do that's the problem. Thinking the problem and the person are one and the same invites more problems. It'll infect your attitude, which will affect your interactions with the employee. It causes unnecessary frustration when you realize you can't change another person. What you can do is influence the employee to want to correct what they're doing—by clearly communicating your expectations, giving feedback, and modeling the behavior you prefer.

base corrective feedback on attitude. You may have done so at one time and had an employee react like this: "My attitude is none of your business. It has nothing to do with the job."

This view that "attitude is none of your business" is incorrect. Attitude has everything to do with how a person performs on the job, because attitude is always acted out. A negative attitude always reveals itself in actions that have negative effects: on the employee's performance, on work group morale, and ultimately on productivity. How an employee acts in the work place is your business.

Although attitude affects performance, don't use the word "attitude" when you give corrective feedback. We tend to equate attitude with our personal sense of self. A comment like "You need to change your attitude" is interpreted to mean "You need to change who you are." Nobody likes hearing that.

To give corrective feedback to someone with a so-called "attitude problem," translate attitude into concrete actions. To prepare for the feedback session, jot down your thoughts as the outline shows (Figure 5-2).

Employee _____

Attitude _____

Actions

Consequences

Figure 5-2. A form to help prepare for a feedback session

How would you describe the employee's attitude? How is that attitude acted out? Make note of the performance-related behavior you've observed that's an outgrowth of their attitude. The consequences of the behavior make clear the reasons to confront the behavior.

Apply These Points

When you give corrective feedback, follow these five guidelines.

1. **Keep It Positive**. Use the "sandwich" technique. Begin with a statement of well-meant intent. End with a positive statement that conveys encouragement or support. Sandwich the corrective feedback between the positive beginning and end.

2. **Do It Promptly**. The sooner the employee receives corrective feedback, the sooner they can start to modify the behavior. Don't save up all of your corrective feedback for an annual performance review and then "unload" on the employee. It's not fair to the employee, it's not fair to their coworkers, and it makes your job tougher if you wait.

3. **Give Feedback in Private**. *Never* correct an employee in the presence of their peers. Always discuss an employee's performance in private.

4. **Do It in Person**. For the record, you may need to document discussions about performance. But the first time an

---

When to Wait

Smart Managing   Employees are human. When beset by unusual circumstances, like a serious personal problem or an exceptionally demanding project at work, people sometimes react in ways they normally don't.

Assess the situation. You may decide to defer giving corrective feedback when:
- the bothersome behavior isn't the norm for this employee
- the consequences of it are nominal
- you have reason to think the behavior will return to normal in time

Keep an eye on the situation. If the behavior doesn't improve but starts to become habitual, then you'll need to confront it. The circumstances may call for an approach that conveys compassionate concern.

employee hears that you have a concern, it ought to come from you, face to face, in person. Don't put a memo in their in-box. Don't send an e-mail. And if you write up an incident or notes from a feedback session, don't send the document to a shared printer where other employees may see it.

There's one exception to the in-person discussion: if you manage personnel who work from remote locations and you don't have occasion to see them on a regular basis. If something needs immediate correction and the matter is routine, then make a telephone call. If the matter is serious (something sufficient for disciplinary action), arrange an in-person meeting.

5. **One Point at a Time**. If an employee does two or three or several things that need to be corrected, begin with the one most important one. Reserve the others for subsequent discussions—after you've seen evidence of improvement on the first one.

Don't bring up several performance issues in one feedback session. Some employees will perceive that you're picking on them. Others will be discouraged because they'll get the feeling that they don't do anything right. And some, after hearing your first point, will tune you out and hear little of what you say after that.

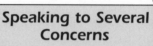

Speaking to Several Concerns

What if an employee repeatedly shows up late for work, returns from lunch late, turns in reports late, and shows up late for meetings? All of those incidents are related to the one issue of timeliness.

When you notice a number of things to be corrected, see if you can group them in one category of performance. Address that one issue and use the several incidents as examples to substantiate your case.

A Format for Giving Corrective Feedback

What's wrong with this picture?

A manager meets with an employee to give corrective feedback and says, "You're so negative you're bringing down the morale of the team. Because of you, we're getting customer complaints. You'd better improve or else."

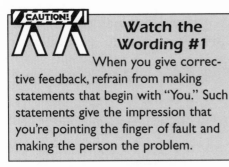

Watch the Wording #1

When you give corrective feedback, refrain from making statements that begin with "You." Such statements give the impression that you're pointing the finger of fault and making the person the problem.

What's wrong is that it's not corrective feedback. It's accusatory feedback. It's derogatory feedback. It's a personalized verbal attack and an implied threat. It doesn't address specific behavior. And there's nothing in what the manager said that would motivate the employee to want to improve their performance.

To effectively communicate corrective feedback, follow these six steps.

1. Start with well-meant intent.
2. Identify the action or behavior to be corrected, and point out the consequences of the behavior.

   Begin by stating, "I ...," such as "I noticed that you ...," "I'm concerned when you ...," or "I've reviewed your work and found ...." (The phrasing "that you" or "when you" refers to what the employee does, as a behavior. It's not the same as saying "you are," as a person.)

3. When it's suitable to the circumstances, pose an open question to create a dialogue and to show that you're receptive to hearing the employee's side of the story. Ask the employee, "What accounts for this?" or "What are the reasons for ...?" Be willing to listen to the employee's explanation.

4. Express your expectation. Clearly communicate what you

Watch the Wording #2

It's a common practice to refer to behavior as "unacceptable" or "inappropriate." If you do, put those words in some context. If you say simply, "This is unacceptable," the employee who reacts may think or even say, "According to who? It's not unacceptable to me." Phrase the point, "According to company policy, it's inappropriate for an employee to ..." or "Everyone on this team agreed it's unacceptable when ..." Of course, in the latter case, make sure that the team has, in fact, agreed to this policy.

need, want, or expect the employee to do differently. Point out positive aspects of making the correction to motivate the employee to want to do it.

Specify a time frame in which you expect the employee's performance to improve. In some cases, you'll say, "From today on, I expect ...." In other situations, it's only fair to give the employee time to improve.

Suppose you manage a plant that produces widgets. An employee is expected to produce 20 widgets a day and currently produces only 10. Say something like "I expect you can reach at least 20 a day by this time next month." Between now and then, have follow-up discussions to communicate appropriate feedback: positive when the employee shows improvement, more corrective feedback if they don't.

5. Ask an open question to elicit a response from the employee. Ask, "How does that sound to you?" or "What are your thoughts about this?"
6. Convey your willingness to work with the employee on improving performance or offer training that will help them correct the behavior.

Here's how the format for giving corrective feedback sounds.

Manager: I understand from conversations we've had that you want to advance in your career. Is that right?"
Gertie: Of course.
Manager: I want to help you achieve your goal, and that's the

---

Watch the Wording #3

Never say "never" or "always," as in "I've noticed you're *always* late for meetings" or "I'm concerned because you *never* comply with safety regulations." "Always" and "never" imply there are no exceptions. Use those words and many employees will find exceptions that prove you wrong. "Always" and "never" also imply it's not likely the employee can or will change—not if they *always* or *never* do something.

Instead of "always," say "often," "frequently," "repeatedly," or "as a rule." Instead of "never," say "rarely" or "infrequently."

reason I'm bringing this up.

I'm aware that you frequently talk about people. When you do that, Gertie, it distracts from the job we're doing and it's potentially hurtful to people you work with.

From today on, instead of talking behind someone's back, I want to you to speak to the person directly. When you do that, Gertie, we'll have a better atmosphere of good communication around here and you'll enjoy more positive working relationships.

How do you feel about that?

Gertie: (Reacts with a look that combines puzzlement and worry.)

Manager: (Responds to reaction, then concludes.) There's a seminar coming up on Professional Communication Skills. It's training you might find useful and it's consistent with your career goals. I'll be glad to approve your enrollment if you want to go.

Let's look at another situation. In this example, the manager is dealing with an employee who has a negative attitude. Notice how no mention is made of attitude. Instead, the manager speaks to a specific behavior.

Manager: I value the years of experience you bring to this job, Ned, and I've noticed you have a knack for spotting problems. We both know that's important in our line of work. It's even more important to come up with solutions, which is the reason I wanted to talk with you.

During team meetings, when someone brings up an idea, often I've heard you say, "It won't work." When you put it that way, it sounds as though you're not willing to consider new ideas. And it has the effect of demoralizing the team.

When you insist an idea won't work, what's your intent, Ned?

Ned: What do you mean, what's my intent?

Manager: I mean, what point are you trying to make when you say an idea won't work?

Ned: Look, I've been around here a lot longer than most of you. I think I know what'll work and what won't work.

Manager: I'm going to take that to mean that you're concerned about the business and you want to see us do the right thing. So do I.

So from today on, here's what I want from you. When someone brings up an idea, give them the benefit of the doubt. If you have a concern about whether it'll work or not, do this. Suggest what needs to be done to make it work. With your experience, Ned, I expect you to come up with solutions.

If you want to run your ideas by me or hash out some possible solutions, I'll be glad to brainstorm with you. How does that sound to you?

Ned: OK, let's try it. I want to be a team player.

For your reference, the six steps to successfully communicate corrective feedback are outlined on the worksheet in Figure 5-3.

Worksheet for Communicating Corrective Feedback

1. **Well-meant intent**

2. **Correction: unsatisfactory performance/behavior**

   Consequences

3. **(Optional) Ask an open question re: explanation**

4. **Expectation: preferred behavior**

   Positive outcomes

5. **Ask an open question to elicit employee response**

6. **Offer encouragement, support, or training**

Figure 5-3. Steps for communicating corrective feedback

Smart Managing

Praise What You Want More Of

When you notice a positive change in the employee's performance—evidence that they're making the correction—express positive feedback. When warranted, positive feedback affirms employees and reinforces their efforts to improve. It also keeps your approach to management balanced. You're not perceived as a "grouch" or a "tyrant" who communicates only when you call employees in to correct them.

How to Respond to Reactions

After you've given an employee corrective feedback, it would be wonderful if they smiled and said, "Thank you for bringing that to my attention. I'll correct it right away." It would be wonderful—and surprising.

Your intent is to offer constructive feedback. But often employees interpret it as criticism. And they react, often defensively.

Be prepared to respond to one or a combination of the following reactions.

1. **Discounts**. The employee shrugs it off. They make light of it, saying something like "It's no big deal. I don't gossip that often and when I do, it doesn't bother anybody. I don't know why you're making such a fuss about it."

Your response: reiterate the reason the behavior needs to be corrected. "Whether it's a little or a lot, gossip is potentially hurtful and distracts from the work at hand. I expect it to stop."

2. **Deflection**. The employee tries to turn your feedback in another direction, away from themselves. They blame someone or something else. "Look, I'm not the only one around here who gossips. Gary gossips worse than I do. He's the one you should talk to."

Your response: refocus on the employee's behavior. "We're discussing *your* performance, Gertie. Have I made it clear that I expect the gossip to stop?"

3. **Defensive**. The employee tries to protect themselves against perceived criticism. They make excuses like "When I say an idea won't work, I'm only trying to be helpful.

Nobody's ever told me it was a problem. I have good ideas for solutions, but nobody ever listens to me."

Your response: reduce their defensiveness and restate the preferred behavior in a positive manner. "I appreciate your trying to be helpful. What will be most helpful to me and to the rest of the team is hearing your ideas for solutions."

If the employee perceives your giving corrective feedback is an attack, their defensiveness may take the form of a counterattack. They turn on you. In an accusing tone of voice, the employee says, "Why are you always picking on me?!"

Don't get defensive in turn. Remain calm and composed. Ask the employee to be specific. Keep putting the ball back in their court with questions.

You: When, exactly, is the last time I picked on you?
Employee: You always do!
You: About what, specifically?
Employee: I don't know. Everything!
You: What do you mean by "everything"?
Employee: Oh, never mind.

The employee will get the message. They can't provoke a reaction from you, and they can't get away with sweeping accusations that have no merit.

4. **Noncommunicative.** When you ask an open question like "How does that sound to you?" the employee says nothing. After receiving corrective feedback, an employee may be noncommunicative for one of two reasons: either they're sulking or they're trying to come to terms with their feelings and aren't sure how to respond.

Ask another open question, like "What are your thoughts about this?" Pause to give the employee time to gather their thoughts. If the employee doesn't answer after 30 seconds (wait at least that long), let them know you're willing to talk with them about the issue. Say, "Let's do this. When you've had a chance to think about this, if you have any questions, come talk to me by this time next week. Otherwise, we'll consider the matter resolved."

Specify a time frame, like within a week. If you don't, some people will stew endlessly. Three months later, they'll burst into your office and want to talk about a matter you thought had been cleared up months before.

No matter how an employee reacts to corrective feedback, as a manager here's what you want to do when you respond.

- Stay focused and stand firm.
- Don't allow the employee's reaction to derail the discussion.
- Reiterate the core point of your corrective feedback.
- Don't get drawn into an argument.

Giving Positive Feedback

According to the renowned American psychologist, William James, "The deepest principle in human nature is the craving to be appreciated."

Look for occasions to express appreciation to employees. Be:

- prompt
- specific
- sincere

Here's how it sounds.

"I appreciate how thoroughly you prepared for the meeting this morning."

"Thank you for working late last night so we could make today's deadline. I appreciate your efforts."

The 80/20 Rule

Smart Managing You're probably familiar with it. Also known as the Pareto Principle, the 80/20 Rule finds an 80-to-20 ratio between causes and effects. Applied to managing employees, it suggests that 80% of performance problems come from 20% of employees. If that's true in your case, are you spending 80% of your time on two out of 10 employees you manage? Give corrective feedback—effectively and consistently—to reduce the time you spend dealing with performance problems. Take care that you don't neglect the positive performers who are producing good results.

"I'm glad I can rely on you for being consistently pleasant with customers. They like it and so do I."

Of the work employees do, some managers have the view, "That's what they get paid for." True. But a little appreciation goes a long way. It's motivating and it helps to build a person's confidence. When you communicate your appreciation, you'll find it instills in people the desire to do their best for you.

> ### In Public or in Private?
>
> A common refrain in management training is "Praise in public. Correct in private." The latter recommendation is solid: when you give corrective feedback, always do so in private. But the former recommendation may be problematic: singling a person out for praise in the presence of others is contrary to some cultural norms.
>
> First, praise the employee in private. Before you give them recognition in front of others, ask if they're comfortable with it.

The Communicator's Checklist for Chapter 5

❑ Communicate instructions clearly and completely. Prepare for what you need to cover, follow the steps to getting good results, and afterwards give feedback and assess your effectiveness.

❑ Confront performance problems to get them corrected.

❑ Follow the six steps for giving corrective feedback effectively.

❑ Respond to employee reactions. Don't react yourself.

❑ Express appreciation.

Dealing with Counterproductive Communications

You begin a meeting with employees. "Paul is here this morning from Human Resources. He'll be telling us about some new features of the benefits package."

Paul: This won't take long. I have three changes to announce that you'll be happy to hear about. First, we've added one more paid holiday to the calendar year.

Sandy: Speaking of holidays, are we having a Founders Day party again this year?

Jane: What I want to know is will the company be expanding its family-friendly policies?

Joe: (in a snide tone of voice) There you go again.

Jane: (offended) What's that remark supposed to mean?

Joe: What it means is—you're the only one around here who cares about it. Trust me, nobody else gives a hoot.

Jane: You care, don't you, Dave?

Dave: (meekly) About what?

Sandy: (cheerfully) Joe, don't you think we should do a party like we did last year?

Jane: (irritated) Could we get back to my question, please?

The meeting takes twice as long as it should. Paul gets through only two of the three items he had to present. And by the time the meeting is over, Joe and Jane aren't talking to each other.

Later, Jane asks to speak with you in your office.

Jane: I'm not going to stand for it anymore. (Tears well up in her eyes.) Joe was so rude to me in the meeting.
You: I can see you're upset.
Jane: Of course I'm upset. (Tearfully) I try to get along with everyone around here and all they do is ... (She's crying.)

On the way home after work, you mull over what you've read about effective communication. Building bridges, you think. I'm supposed to be building bridges of productive working relationships. How on earth do I do that when employees verbally assault one another, take off on tangents, sit in my office crying, or don't speak up at all?

Nobody said bridge building is easy. It does proceed more smoothly, though, when you know how to deal with communication behaviors that are counterproductive.

> **Key Term**
>
> **Counterproductive communications** Communication behavior that does one or more of the following:
> - strains working relationships
> - provokes conflict
> - slows discussion or delays getting the job done
> - stifles the dialogue necessary for group decision making, problem solving, and creative brainstorming
> - creates a negative work environment

Taking Off on Tangents

Picture a lizard lying atop a rock, basking in the sun. If the lizard is startled or if something catches its attention, it leaps off the rock and scurries away. It doesn't take off in a straightforward direction. It darts off unpredictably. You have no idea which way it's going to go.

In this analogy, the rock represents a topic of discussion. When a person takes off on a tangent, they're acting like that lizard. They digress from the topic and bring up an unrelated point. Your objective is to get the "leapin' lizard" back on the rock where it belongs.

Two simple sentences help you do that. "The issue (topic or subject) is not _____ (you fill in the blank). The issue is _____."

When Sandy took off on a tangent, you'd say (courteously, not curtly), "The topic of this meeting is not Founders Day. The topic is the benefits package." To convey that you're willing to consider employees' questions or concerns (even when they're unrelated to the topic at hand), add, "If you want to discuss Founders Day, we can do that at our next meeting or you can talk to me about it after we're finished here." Then refocus the group's attention. Looking at and nodding toward Paul, you'd say, "Paul, go ahead."

Refocusing is especially important when you're talking with an employee about a subject they'd rather not discuss. So they digress.

You: How are you coming along with the month-end report?
Joe: I'm training on this new computer program now. I'll get to the report tomorrow. (Of the many things Joe does on his job, what he likes best is mastering a new computer program.)
You: Joe, we agreed the report was your first priority, and you know it's due to me by noon tomorrow. I need you to put

Send Signals

Smart Managing When a counterproductive communication occurs, you can address it either by saying something or by sending a signal. The benefits of signals are they're brief, good-natured, sometimes humorous. Without sounding like you're harping on it, signals make the point "Let's not do this."

Get employees together to identify communication behaviors that everyone finds counterproductive. Discuss signals to use when these occur. Make sure everyone agrees with the signals so no one takes offense. You might also agree that the person chairing the meeting will normally be the person to send the signal.

off learning the computer program until the report is finished.

Joe: I don't see you telling anyone else how to schedule their work.

You: The issue here is not what I tell others. The issue is getting the report done on time.

What if you're dealing with someone who's an aggressive communicator? Watch out. They'll crank it up a notch or two.

> ## Leapin' Lizards
>
> Here's a signal to use when someone takes off on a tangent. Smile and shout, "Leapin' Lizards!" This assumes, of course, that everyone's familiar with the tale of the lizard leaping off the rock.
>
> One manager I know keeps a rock on the conference table as a centerpiece. When someone takes off on a tangent in a meeting, all anyone has to do is point at the rock. The tangent-taker immediately gets the message: get back to the topic at hand.
>
> Warning: Don't use this signal when the situation doesn't lend itself to humor.

Joe: You're a real (expletive).

Do people really do that? Yes, some do.

Keep your cool. Stand your ground. Maintain your composure, even when you hear hot-button words. A "button pusher" is trying to get a reaction out of you. Don't let them.

You: (calmly) The issue here is not what you think of me. The issue is ...

Joe: I know. I'll get the report done.

In a situation like this, the employee's use of profanity is clearly inappropriate behavior. At the earliest opportunity, you'd give them corrective feedback about it. But not when you're trying to focus on getting the report finished.

When you consistently refocus on the topic at hand, employees eventually learn to refrain from taking off on tangents.

How to Treat Tears

Some people are sensitive. Their emotions run close to the surface. When tears well up in their eyes or they become flushed, they're probably more uneasy about it than you are.

Others use tears as a method of manipulation. They figure you feel awkward when someone cries, so you'll take the quickest way of escape. You'll give in to what they want or postpone the conversation indefinitely (which, in some cases, is what they want).

Here's an effective approach to deal with crying.

1. Acknowledge the person's feelings.
2. Suggest a break. Make it a short break and an unexpected time frame, such as three minutes and 45 seconds. The unusual time frame sounds so ridiculous it can have the effect of reducing the emotion of the moment.
3. Resume your discussion promptly, exactly according to the time frame you specified.
4. If the person starts to cry again, suggest a second break. This time make it shorter, but still odd.
5. If they start to cry again after the second break, offer one of two options: (1) continue the conversation or (2) stop and resume early the next day. Most of the time, people choose to continue the conversation. The genuine crier doesn't want to lie awake worrying about tomorrow morning. And by now, the manipulative crier knows tears don't work to get them what they want.

In the conversation with Jane, here's what you'd do when she started to cry.

You: I can see you're upset. Why don't we take a brief recess and you can regain your composure. I'll see you back here in four minutes and 20 seconds.

The genuine weeper will appreciate your consideration. The manipulator will see that you're retaining control of the situation. Four minutes and 20 seconds later, you continue the conversation.

You: What's on your mind?
Jane: I try to get along with everyone around here and all they do is ... (She starts to cry again.)

You: Jane, let's take a break for three minutes and 10 seconds. Then we'll continue.

Usually, by this point, Jane will say something like "No, I'm OK." Go on with the conversation as though nothing's amiss. If she starts to cry again, offer the two options.

By the way, you may want to keep a box of tissues nearby.

It's Crucial You Stay Calm

It's Crucial You Stay Calm — Smart Managing

Don't let employees' upsets upset you. Emotional reactions are not unusual when conflicts occur between coworkers. They're also more common when excess stress leaves people with a short fuse. It falls to you to be a source of calm.

By your facial expression, tone of voice, and demeanor, convey composure. It's a quality that helps to counteract counterproductive communications.

How to Handle Complaints About Coworkers

Dave steps into your office and asks, "Have you got a minute?" You invite him in. When he closes the door behind him, you know this'll take more than a minute.

Dave is a passive communicator and a chronic complainer. More than anything else he complains about his coworkers.

Dave: You know that project Sandy and I are working on? Well, she took one of my ideas and presented it to the client yesterday as though it was her idea.

Dave stops. He wants you to commiserate with him. Don't. If you do, you'll have Dave taking up your time whenever he's unhappy, which is often.

When an employee voices a complaint about a coworker, ask three questions followed by a statement.

1. "Have you talked to Sandy about this?" He hasn't. Passive communicators are reluctant to speak directly to the person involved.
2. "May I call Sandy in so we can clear up this matter right now?" He says no.

3. "May I talk to Sandy, let her know you've met with me, and tell her what you've told me?" A chronic complainer will answer, "No." They don't want the problem solved. Once it's solved, they'll have nothing to complain about. They want you to assume the role of sympathizer.

A passive communicator will answer, "No" because they want *you* to solve the problem for them. Dave's trying to put the monkey on your back. Put the monkey where it belongs: back on Dave. If you don't, you'll find a lot of your time is taken up settling squabbles among employees that they should be settling themselves.

What if the employee says, "I want you to talk to her. But don't tell her I told you"? Make your position clear: "I'm not willing to do that because this is between you and Sandy. If you want me to get involved, I'll be glad to discuss it with *both* of you, together."

Let the employee know you expect them to solve the problem or take part in solving it. Make a concluding statement like "When you're ready to resolve this situation, let me know" or "I'll be glad to listen when you have a solution to suggest." Use

---

TRICKS OF THE TRADE

Signals for Solutions

Here are a few signals that say, "Let's talk solutions." Before you use any of these, be sure you've first had that discussion with employees about signals everyone agrees to use. Do these with a good-natured smile.

• Point to a motivational poster with a message about solutions. If you can't find one, make one up that reads, "Solutions First" or "We Don't Make Problems—We Make Solutions."

• Keep a statue of the sculpture "The Thinker" on a corner of your desk. Tap the head.

• Pull out of a drawer and place on your desk a prop that serves as a reminder to focus on solutions. A Slinky depicts flexibility. A Rubik's cube signals "Solve this puzzle." A toy fire truck suggests "Let's put out this fire."

Warning: Don't use these or other signals that are meant to be humorous when you're dealing with someone who's upset or communicating aggressively.

the word "when," not "if." "If" implies the employee may or may not want to solve the problem (it's iffy). "When" presupposes that they do want to solve it. It's just a matter of time. "When" expresses a more positive expectation.

With employees who repeatedly voice complaints, consistently communicate an emphasis on solutions.

Aggressive Communications

Like a tornado, Joe storms into your office, slams a stack of printouts on your desk, and shouts, "Look at these! Errors on every page! How can I do my job when the blankety-blank computers in this blankety-blank place don't work?!!"

The veins in his neck are bulging. His fists are clenched. He's bellowing like an enraged bull.

"Those idiots who set up this system don't have a clue. You want that report tomorrow? Well, you're not going to get it unless I can get some decent data. This is outrageous!"

Suppose you say, "Joe, calm down." What does Joe do? He becomes more agitated and shouts even louder, "Don't tell me to calm down!! You don't understand what it takes to do these reports."

You: Yes, I do.

Joe: NO, you don't!

You: (Now you're getting angry.) YES, I DO! I use the same system and I haven't had any problems with it.

Joe: What are you saying? I'm a liar?!!!

Welcome to the world of interacting with aggressive communicators. If they inhabit the world where you work, handle with care.

To interact effectively with aggressive communicators, it helps to understand the underlying needs that trigger their reactions. Typically, aggressive communicators have:

- an inordinate need for control
- the need to be right
- the need to win. They view most situations as a competition. Determined to win, they often resort to intimidating tactics.

These characteristics give you clues of what to do and *not* do when you interact with aggressive communicators.

Don'ts When Dealing with Aggressive Communications

Let's begin with six things you definitely *don't* want to do. If you do these things, the aggressive communicator perceives "you're trying to be right, which will make me wrong, which means I'll lose," or they think you're trying to exert control. In either case, they'll feel their needs are threatened and the forcefulness of their aggressive reaction will increase.

1. **Don't argue.** Arguing with an aggressive communicator adds fuel to the fire. Nothing gets resolved, and often hostilities develop.

2. **Don't tell them how they should think, feel, or be.** No one likes to be told, "Calm down" (i.e., *be* calm). Aggressive communicators *really* don't like it. Refrain from saying things like "You shouldn't feel that way" or "Don't be unreasonable." From statements like that, a person hears you saying that what they're being and thinking and feeling is wrong. Most of us don't like learning we're wrong. Aggressive communicators detest the possibility.

3. **Don't use trite phrases.** Expressions like "When the going gets tough, the tough get going" or "Hang in there" strike aggressive communicators as condescending. When dealing with a person who reacts, you never want to come across as condescending.

4. **Unless you're asked, don't offer advice or propose "the" solution.** To an aggressive communicator, "Here's my advice" or "Let me tell you what I'd do in this situation" sounds like you're trying to exert control. It also implies to them that you think you've got the right answer and they don't.

5. **Don't say anything that hints at being judgmental.** "You're making a mountain out of a molehill" may seem like an innocent comment to you. To an aggressive communicator, it sounds like a put-down.

Stop the Sniping

Smart Managing

Some aggressive communicators use sarcasm as a weapon. In a sneering tone of voice, they make sniping remarks. Put a stop to it. If you allow one person to get away with it, others will pick up the habit, too. And you'll end up trying to manage a group of employees who sling verbal barbs at one another and at you.

When someone snipes, look at them directly. Pause for a moment to get their attention, restate the remark—without the sarcasm—and ask their intent.

You give Aggie an assignment. She says sarcastically, "Oh, this'll work real well." Look directly at her. Pause. Calmly state, "I heard you say, 'This'll work real well.' What do you mean?" Aggie knows you know what she meant. She also knows you won't let her get away with sarcastic sniping. And so does anyone else within earshot.

---

6. **Don't react in kind.** If you react aggressively, the situation will escalate.

Dos to Diffuse Aggressive Communications

You have a twofold objective: to reduce the intensity aggressiveness adds to an interaction and to steer the discussion in a direction that will lead to a favorable outcome. To achieve this objective, use the best of your interpersonal skills, keep your emotions in check, and apply these eight guidelines.

1. **Stay calm.** Emotionally detach yourself from the intensity of the aggressiveness. Recognize it's not aimed at you personally. It wouldn't matter who was sitting in your chair or standing in your place. This is what aggressive communicators do. It's not about you.

   Concentrate on keeping your tone of voice even, your rate of speech measured, and your facial expression impassive. Respond in short sentences in a matter-of-fact manner.

2. **Initially, let them vent.** Don't interrupt to comment on what they're saying. An aggressive communicator is wound up. When you allow them to let off steam, the intensity of their reaction will start to run down.

   Don't try to talk them out of their irritation, frustration, or anger. The more you talk, the more the aggressive communicator senses that you're trying to take over. Or they'll think you're being argumentative. That may not be your intent, but it's how they'll interpret it.

3. **Acknowledge the situation.** Use statements like "I can see how that would be frustrating" or "It's unfortunate this happened." Express empathy—but don't voice agreement.

If you agree with Joe, "You're right. This is a blankety-blank system," Joe will take it to mean that he's right being angry about the system. He'll also take it to mean that he's right to react the way he does.

4. **Make a "safe" response.** Early on, say something succinct like "Tell me more," "Fill me in on the details," or "Go on." These are "safe" because they don't instigate further aggressiveness. Aggressive communicators usually don't expect such a response so it catches them off guard.

Joe said, "This is outrageous!" What if, instead of saying, "Calm down," you said, "Tell me more"? There's nothing in that to provoke a reaction. You're showing your willingness to listen. And you're putting the ball in Joe's court.

The longer aggressive communicators talk, the more likely it is they'll start to run out of steam. The more they say, the more insight you gain to discern the crux of the matter.

5. **Focus on the core concern.** Aggressive communication behaviors are so strong that it's easy to get caught up in or distracted by them. They tend to mask what the shouter is ranting about. Focus on getting past the aggressive behaviors. Listen for clues to what's really on the person's mind.

Joe complains about errors in the data. He faults the computer system. What's he getting at? What's the underlying issue? You may remember he said, "You want that report tomorrow? Well, you're not going to get it unless ..." Joe's real concern is missing the report deadline.

In this type of incident, it's helpful to know the work habits of the employees you manage. Does Joe plan his time and workload well or poorly? Is "thriving on chaos" and "putting out fires" his usual mode? Or is his concern about the computer system valid? What you know will help you decide how to respond.

6. **Ask "what" and "how" questions.** "What do *you* think we ought to do?" "How do *you* suppose we should handle this?" (Put a slight bit of emphasis on "you.") Such questions suggest you're seeking their input, which gives aggressive communicators a sense of control.

The "I'm Looking to Understand" Look

Every dog owner is familiar with this look. It's the way a pet looks at its owner to pick up visual cues. It's not a stare or a glare. It's a focused, unblinking, and mildly curious gaze. The dog sits quietly and looks at its owner with concentrated interest.

While an aggressive communicator is talking, look at them with a similar expression. It suggests, "You've got my attention. I'm looking to understand." It appeals to their need for control. And it keeps you from trying to outtalk them.

Remember: after asking a question, wait for the answer. The silence that follows your question can have a calming effect. Get comfortable with sitting still. If you think about it, it makes sense. Until the aggressive communicator's frame of mind is conducive to hearing what you have to say, you have nothing to gain by talking.

7. **Use provisional statements.** Phrased "If ..., then ...," the statement makes this provision: *if* you'll let me speak, *then* you'll get your turn. In other words, you're letting the aggressive communicator know they'll get back a point of control.

When you're speaking, if an aggressive communicator interrupts (which they're prone to do), say, "If you'll let me finish, then I'll give you my undivided attention." When you want to make a point, try this: "If you'll allow me to offer a suggestion, then I'll be glad to hear what you think about it."

8. **Set limits.** Sometimes your use of interpersonal skills will help diffuse the situation. Perceiving that you're listening and willing to give them their due, the aggressive communicator will calm down and you can continue the conversation in a more moderate manner. Sometimes. Not always.

Some aggressive communicators keep it up and exceed the bounds of barely acceptable behavior. Then you must make absolutely clear that "this" will not be tolerated. "This" is verbal abuse, profanity, and excessive actions that appear threatening. Specify the unacceptable behavior.

As soon as Joe slammed the printouts on the desk, you'd say firmly (without raising your voice), "Stop. I'm willing to listen to what you have to say, Joe. I am *not* willing to listen when you slam things on my desk and shout. Now let's start over."

Notice the word "but" doesn't appear between the sentences "I'm willing to ..." and "I am not willing to ...." Don't use "but" when talking to aggressive communicators. To them, "but" means you didn't mean the first thing you said.

If someone uses profanity, as Joe did when he referred to the "blankety-blank computer," immediately break in and say assertively, "Joe, if you want me to hear you out, I'm going to ask you to *not* use profanity. I find it offensive and I won't tolerate it in this office. Now, what were you saying about the system?"

Notice how these two examples of setting limits are worded. They're phrased to convey that the assertive communicator has a choice. It's as though you're saying, "Do you want me to listen or not? You decide. If you do, don't slam things and don't use foul language." Given a choice, aggressive communicators retain a sense of control.

When interacting with aggressive communicators, be assertive. Maintain a moderate, yet firm manner.

If you're passive, aggressive communicators will succeed in intimidating you. Having succeeded once, they'll do it again and again.

If you react aggressively, you give them an excuse to be aggressive, too. You can't expect employees to be calm and reasonable if you aren't. You can't ask them to observe the limits of constructive communications if you don't.

Watch the Level of Aggressiveness

If an employee habitually exhibits aggressive communication behaviors, give them corrective feedback about it. If their aggressiveness continues or escalates, consider enrolling the employee in anger management training or refer them to an Employee Assistance Program.

An aggressive communicator may, in the extreme, voice a threat (implied or explicit) or display threatening behavior. Never counter a threat with a threat. Never take a threat lightly. Know your organization's policies regarding how to respond to threats. As a precaution, promptly report any incident of threatening behavior to the human resources or security department.

To Ease Explosive Behaviors

Explosive outbursts look and sound like aggressiveness. But people who *occasionally* react explosively are not aggressive communicators by nature or as a norm. Their apparent aggressiveness erupts spontaneously when something is said that sets them off.

In a problem-solving discussion, Ellie offers a suggestion. Cal mutters (loud enough for everyone to hear), "That's a half-baked idea if I ever heard one." Kaboom! Ellie explodes. "What do you mean 'half-baked'? I don't hear you coming up with any ideas!" Unless you intervene, she'll go on and on.

When this type of explosive behavior occurs, here's what you want to do.

- Affirm the person. People who are intermittently explosive tend to be sensitive or insecure. They need a boost to their confidence. Say something like "Ellie, I'm pleased by the way you participate in discussions. You've come up with many good ideas."
- Call a break to allow time for emotions to subside. Be careful how you word it. Don't say, "Let's take a break so you can cool off." (That could set off another explosion.) Say, "Let's take a break for a few minutes to give this idea more thought."

- Identify what it is that "trips their trigger." What set Ellie off? The phrase "half-baked," which she took as a personal criticism. Most explosions can be prevented by refraining from caustic, critical, or sarcastic remarks.

Passive Communications

You're meeting with the team to discuss how to speed up processing job orders. Several employees offer useful suggestions. Patti's job will be most affected by a change and you're concerned because she doesn't speak up.

Patti is a passive communicator. After Arturo brought up an idea, you asked Patti, "How does that sound to you?" "Fine," she answered. Sandy made a suggestion, then said to Patti, "You're the one who inputs the orders. Do you think you could do it this way instead?" Patti smiled and nodded, "Sure." But you're not sure she's saying what she really thinks.

After the meeting, you talk with Patti.

You: How did you feel about the meeting today?
Patti: OK.
You: A lot of ideas came out, but I didn't hear you express an opinion. Is anything wrong?
Patti: No.
You: Which idea did you like best?
Patti: (After a long silence) Um, I don't know.
You: (Growing frustrated and impatient) Patti, what do you want to do on this?
Patti: Anything's fine with me. I'll do whatever makes everyone else happy.

It's the kind of response you'd expect. Passive communicators don't want to make waves, rock the boat, ruffle anyone's feathers. They don't want to risk saying or doing anything that might disappoint or upset someone else. So they tend to say little.

When passive communicators do speak up, generally it's in a meek manner. And they'll quickly back down if someone questions or objects to what they've said.

How do you interact effectively with passive communicators? Start by understanding their needs for:

- reassurance
- approval
- harmony in relationships

Don'ts When Dealing with Passive Communicators

These needs suggest three things you don't want to do when dealing with passive communicators.

1. **Don't come on too strong.** If you tend to be a confident and assertive communicator, tone it down. Purposely take a more tentative approach.

   If you're inclined to be an aggressive communicator, curb the inclination. The more intimidating your communication behaviors, the more uncommunicative the passive person will become. They won't open up and be honest with you. The building could be on fire and they wouldn't say anything for fear of upsetting you.

2. **Don't come across as critical.** Passive communicators want to be liked. They want to please people. And they often feel personally crushed if it sounds like someone is blaming or finding fault with them.

3. **Don't be abrupt or rushed.** Typically, passive communicators take more time to formulate an idea or an answer to a question. They want to be sure it'll be a "good" idea or the "right" answer—the one you'll like.

In your conversation with Patti, you asked, "Which idea did you like best?" There was a long silence from Patti. Refrain from saying something like "C'mon, Patti, I haven't got all day." A passive communicator would perceive they're at fault for holding you up.

Dos for Dealing with Passive Communicators

When interacting with passive communicators, your objective is to prompt them to speak up. To do that, follow these five guidelines.

Getting an Answer

You ask a question and a passive communicator answers, "I don't know." What do you do? Training professional Michael Staver suggests this simple but effective technique. Ask, "If you did know, what would your answer be?"

Because it's unexpected and somewhat humorous, it helps to put the passive communicator at ease. If they continue to be reluctant to speak up and insist, "I said I don't know," appeal to their desire to please. "Help me out here. What's your best guess?"

1. **Be congenial.** Speak in a mild-mannered tone of voice. Appear pleasant and patient; smile if it's appropriate to the situation. Project a sense of being at ease. It'll help put the passive communicator at ease, too.

2. **Create an empathetic connection.** Communicate your interest in understanding their anxieties or concerns. Use expressions like "If I were in your shoes ..." and "When I did a job similar to this, I felt ...."

   In the conversation with Patti it would sound like this: "Patti, if I were in your shoes, I might feel a bit confused by all of the ideas that came up. Is that how you're feeling?"

3. **Express reassurance.** Use phrases like "You can be sure ...," "I hope you know you can ...," and "I'm confident ...." Encourage their input with statements like "I want you to know I welcome any questions you have; there's no such thing as a dumb question" or "I value your ideas and I want to hear them."

   Talking with Patti, you might interject statements like these: "I hope you know you can speak openly with me," "You can be sure I'll be glad to hear your opinion on this," "I'm confident you have something useful to add to the discussion," "I'd like to hear what you have to say."

4. **Ask open questions to prompt a response.** Look expectant while you wait for the answer. Lean forward slightly. If need be, rephrase the question and ask again. "Which idea did you like best?" might be restated to ask, "In your opinion, Patti, what idea would be most workable?"

5. **Convey accountability.** If you still can't get the passive communicator to speak up, make a statement that clearly conveys, "ultimately, you're responsible." To emphasize their accountability, use the phrase "you leave me no recourse."

> "Patti, you can let me know what you think about this or not. If you don't let me know, you'll leave me no recourse but to make the decision without your input." Pause to allow them a moment to reconsider and, you hope, speak up. If they still say nothing, continue, "If you don't speak up, I'll expect you to accept whatever impact the decision has on your job."

Your Role in Conflict Between Employees

According to the *Journal of Business Communication*, the most frequently cited source of interpersonal conflict in an organization is poor communication. From the previous discussion of counterproductive communications, you can see how such behaviors could provoke conflicts between coworkers.

Conflict is a fact of life. It's bound to happen. Look around the group of employees you manage and you'll notice natural differences in:

- attitudes
- expectations
- interpretations of events
- perceptions of one another
- communication profiles and preferences
- age, gender, ethnic background, and cultural norms

Such differences produce differences of opinion, which can lead to conflict.

Conflict may be a fact of life, but you don't want it to become a way of life. A work group bogged down in continual conflict is just that—bogged down.

Conflict can be either constructive or destructive. Conflict is *constructive* when:

- it gets people talking
- it brings to light valid concerns
- it ushers in creative brainstorming
- the resolution of the conflict results in an improvement

Conflict is *destructive* and counterproductive when:

- it becomes personal
- employees are pitted against one another
- it adds stress and negativity to the work environment
- issues aren't resolved; they're suppressed, recur, recycle, and raise hostilities.

When counterproductive conflict occurs between coworkers, there are three roles you might fill.

1. *Participant.* Do *not* step into this role. Refrain from entering the fray and becoming embroiled in the conflict.
2. *Arbitrator.* Avoid this role. As an arbitrator, you'd listen to each employee's views and weigh the respective pros and cons. You'd make the final decision about how the dispute will be settled. Clearly, there are drawbacks to doing so.

   Feeling it was imposed upon them from "outside," employees aren't inclined to embrace an arbitrated decision. They have little reason to take ownership of your solution. You may be seen as taking one side against another and perhaps accused of favoritism. If the decision creates a "win/lose" situation, the "loser" won't like it and may resent you. And you end up with an employee-manager conflict to resolve.
3. *Facilitator.* This is your role. As a facilitator, you mediate discussions and guide the employees to resolve their conflict themselves.

Functions of a Facilitator

Assist in moving the process forward toward a mutually satisfactory solution. Refrain from jumping in and taking over. Your role is to help out (with the emphasis on *help*). Help the employees:

1. Establish ground rules for their discussions.

Don't Intervene Without an Invitation

Smart
Managing

When you become aware of a conflict between employees, watch to see if they're working through it and getting it resolved on their own. If they're not, offer your assistance.

"I know it's important to you to get this matter settled. May I help out?"

"I'm concerned that this is getting out of hand. Would you be willing to let me work with you on it?"

As you facilitate the employees' problem-solving discussions, demonstrate conflict resolution skills they can use in the future should other conflicts arise.

2. Isolate and define the issue at the core of the conflict, by posing open questions to elicit each person's view.
3. State their respective positions on the issue.
4. Identify interests they have in common, such as mutual goals, completing interdependent tasks, getting the job done well.

When a conflict occurs, here's the key to getting it resolved. Guard against people becoming polarized on their respective positions.

Direct discussions to find and focus on interests the employees have in common.

When people keep in mind their common interests, discussions will be more reasonable and a mutually agreeable resolution more likely.

1. Ask a lot of "What if?" questions to prompt employees to think about multiple options. Encourage them to consider various possibilities for resolving the issue.
2. Listen attentively. When necessary, to avoid confusion or misunderstanding, restate a point to clarify it.
3. Recap the key points of each discussion.
4. Confirm the agreement the employees have reached.
5. Help them develop a plan and schedule to implement their solution.
6. Ask the employees to set a date when they'll report to you on their progress.

Follow up to ensure that the conflict is indeed resolved. When it is, commend them on their success in resolving the conflict in a reasonable and productive manner.

The Communicator's Checklist for Chapter 6

❑ Deal with counterproductive communications calmly and assertively.

❑ Use constructive communication skills to deal with tangents, tears, and coworker complaints.

❑ Follow the Dos and Don'ts for interacting effectively with aggressive and passive communicators.

❑ Function as a facilitator to help employees resolve their conflicts.

Making the
Most of Meetings

A s a manager, you're responsible for and involved in many things. Giving thought to all you do, fill in the blanks below to complete this statement:

An effective manager:

_____

_____

_____

_____

_____

Does your list include "makes the most of meetings"?

Managers often overlook the potential of meetings. Meetings are an opportunity to carry out many of the things you need to do to be effective. Through meetings, you can direct, inform, and motivate employees. You can strengthen the cohesiveness of your team. You can help to hone employees' critical-thinking skills and tap into their insights and experience to get problems solved. You can observe employees' interactions with their peers and their conduct in a group setting. And you can demonstrate your leadership skill. You can accomplish all of this through meetings—but only if you do them well.

For all of their potential benefit, meetings also consume time: your time and the time of the employees you manage. Since management is about producing results through others, with every meeting we ought to ask two crucial questions: Will this meeting be a productive use of our time? Will it reap results?

The Cost/Benefit Ratio

Before you call a meeting, calculate its estimated cost. You can quickly get a rough estimate by figuring:

Number of people attending	_____
x average hourly cost per person	_____
= Cost per hour	_____
x time in the meeting	_____
+ time/cost to prepare	_____
+ materials	_____
+ refreshments	_____
Total Estimated Cost	_____

Weigh the cost against the benefits you anticipate from the meeting. Note the value you expect in these terms:

As a result of this meeting, I will gain _____. Employees attending will gain _____. As a team or work group, we'll gain _____ or produce _____.

Do the results you anticipate from the meeting justify its time and cost?

If more managers considered these cost/benefit factors, there'd be fewer meetings. And those meetings would be planned better and conducted more skillfully.

The first step in planning for an effective meeting is to consider the type of meeting.

Types of Meetings

What's true of every meeting? Communication occurs. But the nature of the communication varies depending upon the type of meeting.

Meetings fall into one of two categories: presented and participative.

> ### Is There Another Way?
> **Smart Managing**
>
> You're thinking of calling a meeting. First consider if there's a more time-efficient and cost-effective way to accomplish what you'd do in the meeting. Can you communicate the same information to employees in written form: by a memo, report, or bulletin board announcement? Can you make the decision yourself or in a mini-meeting with one or two others?

Presented Meetings

These are meetings in which communication is primarily one-way: from meeting leader to those in attendance. Two types of meetings fall into this category: *informational* and *motivational*.

Assuming you're leading the meeting, you deliver the message or call on others to present information. You or other presenters have the active role. Attendees play a comparatively passive role. In an informational meeting, they may ask questions. In a motivational meeting, they may applaud. But most of the time, they're listening (you hope).

The success of the meeting relies heavily on your presentation skills (discussed in the next chapter).

Participative Meetings

Two types of meetings commonly fall into this category: *problem-solving* and *brainstorming*. In these meetings, everyone participates. Ideally, no one person dominates the discussion. Communication consists of an exchange of ideas. Although you may use brainstorming techniques in a problem-solving meeting, there are differences between the two types.

A problem-solving meeting is held, obviously, to solve an existing problem. The atmosphere tends to be more serious, the format of the meeting more structured, and the approach more analytical. The objective is to reach a decision about how to correct the situation and keep it from recurring. Sometimes such meetings might address an anticipated problem and how to minimize or prevent it from happening—always better than having to solve a problem after it's occurred.

In a brainstorming meeting, the group is focused on improvement. The meeting is occasioned by an interest in innovation or planning for the future. The format of a brainstorming session is more free form, the approach is creative, and the atmosphere ought to be fun because a sense of playfulness stimulates creative thinking. The objective is to generate fresh ideas and choose which will be adopted.

In participative meetings, employees assume an active role. Your role is to direct their discussion. The success of problem-solving and brainstorming meetings relies largely on your facilitation skills.

Logistics

Many managers delegate logistics to a secretary or meeting planner. These include such tasks as reserving a meeting room and arranging for handouts, visual aids, and refreshments.

If you delegate these tasks, communicate the type of meeting, its purpose, and the kind of climate you want to create. Don't overlook lighting, noise factors, the seating arrangement, the general atmosphere of the meeting room, and the choice of refreshments. These have an impact on the energy and attentiveness of a group and the ease with which participants interact.

"Musts" Before a Meeting

Before a meeting even begins, you communicate unspoken messages to employees about the meeting and your management style. From your planning and preparation—or lack of it—employees form an impression about the importance of the meeting and the experience they can expect.

Compare two scenarios. In the first, on Wednesday afternoon a manager hurriedly sends an e-mail to all employees: "Mtg tomorrow 10 am Conf rm." In the second scenario, on Monday morning a manager distributes to all employees a printed memo or an e-mail: "Please arrange your schedules to attend the following meeting.

Date: Thursday, 6/16
Time: 10 a.m. to 11:30 a.m.
Location: Conference Room B
Purpose: Decide on Quality Control Measures
Attached: Agenda and report on Topic A
Please review the report before the meeting and come pre-
pared to discuss it."

What does each scenario tell employees? Which meeting
would you take more seriously and better prepare for? Which
would you expect will have greater value for the time you'll
spend in the meeting?

Certainly, there are times when a situation calls for a spontaneous meeting. If an unexpected problem erupts, you may need
to call an on-the-spot meeting to "put out the fire." But such
occasions should be the exception rather than the rule. If you
have a lot of fires, this is symptomatic of deeper problems in
the organization.

As a rule, you'll get better results from a meeting that's well-
prepared. So beforehand, determine:

- Purpose
- Plan
- Participants

Purpose

The purpose of a meeting
is, of course, related to its
type. But for a specific
meeting, state its specific
purpose.

State it in a way that
zeroes in on the result(s)
you want the meeting to
produce. Here's a useful
way to state the purpose of
a meeting: "By the end of
this meeting, participants

**Not "Why?" but "For
What Purpose?"**   Smart
Managing
Ask some managers the
purpose of a meeting and they'll
answer, "We always have a staff meeting on Tuesday morning." That statement answers the question, "Why are
you holding this meeting?" It does not
answer the question, "For what purpose?"

If you don't have a purpose for a
meeting more meaningful than "We've
always done it this way," don't hold
the meeting.

will _____." For an informational meeting, for example, the purpose might be stated this way: "By the end of this meeting, employees will follow the new procedures for data security."

A clear statement of purpose and expected results helps you determine other planning aspects of the meeting, like how long the meeting needs to be and who should attend. When you open the meeting, it helps you communicate the purpose with clarity for the benefit of the group. It helps you keep the meeting on track as you facilitate the discussion. And soon after it's over, you'll know if the meeting served its purpose.

The Plan

The purpose of a meeting determines your plan, which is the agenda for the meeting.

An agenda communicates:

- what topics will be covered
- how long you plan to spend on each topic or lead the discussion
- who's going to present each topic

Figure 7-1 illustrates a sample agenda.

Sample Agenda				
Time	**Topic**	**Method**	**By**	**Outcome**
1:15-2:00	Marketing Plan	Discussion		
2:00-2:15	June results	Presentation	AKA	
2:15-2:25	Break			
2:25-3:00	Advertising campaign	Brainstorm/ discussion		Start on new plan
3:00-3:10	Forward actions	Discussion		Decision on who does what
3:10-3:20	Review meeting	Round robin		

Figure 7-1. A sample agenda of a well-planned meeting

An agenda would seem a simple thing to "throw together." That's exactly what some managers do: throw it together without much thought. And they end up with a poorly planned meeting that's not as effective as it could be.

When you plan the agenda for a meeting, follow these guidelines.

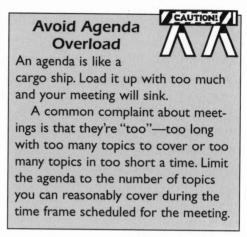

Avoid Agenda Overload

An agenda is like a cargo ship. Load it up with too much and your meeting will sink.

A common complaint about meetings is that they're "too"—too long with too many topics to cover or too many topics in too short a time. Limit the agenda to the number of topics you can reasonably cover during the time frame scheduled for the meeting.

Specify topics. Limit the agenda to topics that support the purpose of the meeting. Some meetings will consist of one topic only; others may include several.

Since attentiveness tends to be highest at the beginning of a meeting, put the highest-priority topic first. If your meetings must follow rules of order that require addressing "old business" first, get through it quickly.

For each topic indicate how you will approach it: for example, roundtable discussion, brainstorm, or presentation followed by discussion. This helps participants properly prepare for their role in the meeting.

Always end a meeting on a high note. You want people leaving a meeting feeling good about the experience. So put last on the agenda a topic that's uplifting: something exciting, humorous, energizing, or motivating.

Set time frames. Allot time to each topic, proportionate to the relative importance of the topic.

Take care that you don't plan an agenda that's too tight: too many topics with too little time to adequately cover each one. You'll give the impression of rushing through the agenda. Participants will have little "breathing space" to assimilate the information or shift mental gears. You'll risk running late, or the last topic or two will get dropped or put off until the next meeting—which may make the agenda for that meeting tight.

Don't spend so much time on a topic that participants get bored and the meeting bogs down. After 45 minutes on the same subject, attention and retention lag. Unless the atmosphere of a meeting is *very* lively, after an hour you'll lose most people. They may be in the meeting room physically, but mentally they'll drift off.

Bearing those factors in mind, plan brief breaks at least every 45 to 60 minutes. Even a 30-second stand-and-stretch break helps people perk up. Periodically, inject some change of pace or approach. Break from presenting information to involving participants. Ask them to write out questions or comments on the topic or to discuss key points with the person seated next to them.

Build cushion into the agenda. Frequently, topics take more time than you initially estimate. If you think a topic can be covered in 35 minutes, allocate 40 or 45 minutes to it. Meeting leaders ad-lib. Participants interrupt with questions and comments. Cushions of extra time allow for these things. If the extra time isn't used, the worst that'll happen is you'll end the meeting early. (Many people think that's the *best* thing that could happen.)

Invite input. If you hold regular staff meetings, welcome employees' suggestions for topics they'd like included on the agenda. It makes it "their" meeting, not just yours.

Best Times to Meet

Smart Managing   Studies on our sleep-wake cycle suggest certain times are better than others for meetings.

Typically, we have two "peak" periods when our physical energy and mental alertness are highest. For people who work days, those times are about 9:30-11:30 in the morning and about 3:00-5:00 in the afternoon. Most people experience a "slump" between 1:00 and 3:00 p.m.

During peak times it's best to schedule those high-priority meetings that require mental agility (like problem-solving and brainstorming sessions). It's best not to schedule routine staff meetings during peak times, not if doing so takes employees away from higher-priority tasks.

Refrain from holding meetings on Monday mornings and Friday afternoons. At those times, employees are often preoccupied with other concerns.

Employees' suggestions also communicate to you issues or concerns they have on their minds.

Distribute the agenda ahead of time. Whenever possible, distribute the agenda to participants at least two or three days before the meeting. Help people come to the meeting well prepared. Attach to the agenda materials you want them to review before the meeting. When you express the expectation that employees show up for meetings prepared, and it becomes the norm, you can accomplish more in less time.

Participants

If you're like many people, you've had this experience. You're sitting in a meeting thinking, "I don't need to be here. This is a waste of my time." Not everyone needs to attend every meeting.

Determine who should attend based on the purpose of the meeting and the topics on the agenda. If you're going to cover three or four topics, and only one of them concerns all employees, put that one topic first on the agenda. After this first topic is covered, excuse those who don't need to stay for the rest of the meeting.

> **Key Term**
>
> **Participant** A person who takes part in an activity or shares in a common experience. Participation is key to the value employees gain from a meeting. In every type of meeting, think of those present not as employees or attendees, but as *participants*. Doing so encourages you to engage employees. In presented meetings, present the content in a manner that engages their attention and interest so employees participate mentally, if not more actively. In participative meetings, get everyone involved in contributing input and responding to ideas.

In planning a meeting, assign roles. Here are some common roles that help meetings run smoothly.

Leader. Every meeting needs a leader. This person opens the meeting, states the purpose, introduces the agenda, oversees the meeting to keep it on track, and closes the meeting. If you normally occupy the role of leader, have in mind one or two high-readiness employees who can fill in for you in case you're absent or running late.

Facilitator. This role is essential in participative meetings. It requires good interpersonal skills, particularly the ability to facilitate discussions and to guide the group successfully through the brainstorming or problem-solving process. The meeting leader usually fills this role or delegates it to a high-readiness employee who has good facilitation skills.

Presenter. This role may be carried out by the meeting leader or assigned to others. When you ask someone to present a topic at a meeting, confirm with them the objective of their presentation to ensure that it coincides with the purpose of the meeting. State your expectation that they'll be well prepared to present effectively. Too often, presenters try to wing it at the last minute and it shows.

Make clear to presenters the time frame allotted to their topic. Insist they adhere to it. Nothing can throw off an agenda faster than presenters who run over their allotted time. If the first presenter takes 10 minutes longer, and the next presenter exceeds their time by 10 minutes, by the time you get to the third topic you have three choices: cut short the topic, eliminate it from the agenda, or let the meeting run late. It's a choice you shouldn't have to make.

Timekeeper. Because of a tendency to lose track of time, it's helpful to have someone "watch the clock." When you're leading or facilitating a meeting, you want your mind free to focus on the topic at hand and the dynamics of the group discussion. So don't take on watching the time yourself. Assign this role.

Ask the timekeeper to send you (or a presenter) two or three signals. "Ten fingers up" indicates 10

What to Say When Time's Running Out

When the time allotted to a topic is running low, let people know. Say something like "If we're going to stick to the agenda, we need to wrap up our discussion in 10 minutes." "We have five minutes before we move on to the next topic. Do we need to take more time than that?" "Can we come to a conclusion now, or do we need to schedule a follow-up meeting?"

minutes remain on the time allotted to the topic. "Five fingers up" signals only five minutes to go. When the time's up, use a "time-out" signal.

Recorder. In formal settings, this person records a complete set of minutes of a meeting. In informal settings, this person takes notes of key discussion points, tasks assigned, and decisions reached. An easy way to do this is to use the format of "One-Minute Minutes" shown in Figure 7-2. Prepare the form on standard letter-size paper.

One-Minute Minutes			
Team/Dept. _____ **Meeting Date** _____			
Agenda Item _____			
Discussion Points _____			
_____			
Decision _____			
Task/To Do	**Assigned to**	**Due Date**	**Form of Reporting**
			❏ to management ❏ memo to participants ❏ next meeting

Figure 7-2. A form for one-minute minutes

Before the meeting, the recorder makes a copy of this form for each agenda item and then enters the meeting and agenda information on the form. During the meeting, the recorder makes key word notes on the form. After the meeting, the recorder immediately copies the "One-Minute Minutes" and distributes them to all participants.

An easier way to do "One-Minute Minutes" is to set up a template on a laptop computer. The recorder enters notes on the keyboard and then prints them off after the meeting.

> ### Rotate and Delegate
>
> **Smart Managing** Whenever possible, delegate meeting roles as a way to:
> • develop employees
> • encourage employees to take ownership of the meeting
> • get employees actively involved in the meeting
> • relieve yourself from having to assume all of the responsibilities
>
> Rotate the assignment of roles. Refrain from delegating the same roles to the same people all of the time. With some roles, like time-keeper and recorder, you may be seen as "dumping" on people. With other roles, like leader and presenter, you may be perceived as playing favorites.

Keeping Meetings on Time and on Track

It's an all too familiar story. A meeting is scheduled to start at 10:00 a.m. Most employees are in the room by 10:15, but some are still standing around the coffee pot. The meeting starts late. It's disrupted by an even later latecomer who shows up at 10:30 and asks, "What did I miss?"

One or two participants monopolize the discussion. A few don't speak up at all. Two or three are carrying on a conversation on the side. Someone answers their cell phone.

Midway through the meeting you call for a 15-minute break. You're lucky if everyone's back after 25 minutes.

As you draw the meeting to a close, you schedule a follow-up session because of "unfinished business." Since the purpose of this meeting wasn't achieved, another meeting is needed. And when the group meets again next week, the same situation recurs.

Start on Time

No excuses. If you've notified employees that a meeting is scheduled to start at 10:00, start at 10:00. If no one's shown up by then, start anyway, just as though everyone were present. You may get a few odd looks from people as they arrive late and notice you're speaking to an empty room. But they'll get the message: next time, show up on time.

Starting meetings on time is important for these reasons:

- *People plan their schedules around meetings.* For employees who show up on time, the 10 or 20 minutes they have to wait until the meeting starts is wasted. Meetings that start late often end late, throwing off everyone's schedule for the rest of the day.

  Delays waste time, a valuable resource. Think back to the calculations you did to estimate the cost/benefit ratio. How much does it cost the company to delay starting a meeting just five or 10 minutes?

- *Waiting to start until latecomers arrive conveys a lack of regard for those who were present to start on time.* It says to latecomers, "It's OK to be late. We'll wait for you." It says to those who arrive on time, "You're less important than those who arrive late."

- *Delays will grow longer and longer.* If you allow meetings this month to start 10 minutes late, next month they'll start 15 minutes late. The month after that, it'll be 20 minutes, and so on. The day will come when you'll be so annoyed by how late meetings start, you'll write a memo, send an e-mail, set a policy, and post a bulletin board notice insisting that meetings start on time. And everyone will wonder, "What's the boss so upset about? We *always* start late."

What do you do in a situation like this? An employee comes up to you after the meeting and says, "Sorry I was late, boss. What did you cover the first 20 minutes?" Smile and reply, "Check with one of your coworkers. Ask them to fill you in." You want the latecomer to get the message, "I'm holding you accountable. You work

A Common Complaint

Employees ask, "What if it's the boss who's always late?" Hold yourself to the same expectations you have for employees. If you expect *them* to be on time, *you* need to be on time. What if you're unavoidably delayed? If you've delegated the role of meeting leader, direct the person to start on time even if you're not there yet. Or have in mind a "second in command" who can get the meeting going until you arrive.

it out." It won't take too many incidents like this before coworkers tire of having to bring the coworker up to date. After a while, latecomers learn to show up on time.

Set Ground Rules

Meetings, even free-form brainstorming sessions, need some structure to stay on track. Ground rules establish norms everyone's expected to observe in meetings.

Rather than mandate the ground rules yourself, this is a good task to delegate to employees. Ask for a few volunteers to form a meeting task force to develop ground rules for the group. A typical list would include:

- Show up on time.
- Come prepared.
- Stick to the agenda.
- One person to speak at a time. No interrupting.
- No hogging the floor. Address one point, then give someone else a chance.
- Don't be a distraction: no cross-talk, sidebar conversations, or cell phone calls while the meeting is under way.
- Show courtesy and respect to others.
- Return from breaks promptly.

Ask the task force to present the ground rules at a meeting. Welcome additional suggestions from others. And for every meeting, have the ground rules posted on the door or by the coffee.

Back from Breaks

When you call a break, clearly state:

- the time: "It's 11:00."
- the length of the break: "We'll take a break for 15 minutes."
- when the meeting will resume: "We'll start up again promptly at 11:15."

A minute or two before the meeting's due to resume, check the room. If many people aren't back in their seats yet, send a signal. Flicker the lights. If necessary, announce that the meeting is going to resume. Make sure that people who might go check messages do so quickly or wait until the meeting is over to do this.

Stay on Track with a Process

In problem-solving meetings, follow a logical and sequential process. Make sure all participants are familiar with the process.

One such process progresses through four steps.

How to Handle Being Held Up

TRICKS OF THE TRADE

Are your meetings held up because people are slow to arrive or return from breaks? Ask your meeting task force to come up with some amusing "penalties" like these. The last person to enter the meeting room will be the last one to leave: they have to clean up and put the room in order. Latecomers get "KP" for a week: they have to clean the kitchen area in the break room. Latecomers will be called on to recap key points of a topic. Keep the "penalties" lighthearted and make sure everyone agrees so no one's embarrassed or offended. And make sure that the penalties apply to anybody, regardless of position.

---

1. Define the problem.
2. Diagnose the problem. The "fishbone technique" (shown in Figure 7-3) is one approach. The center line signifies the problem; the diagonal lines represent components of the problem or contributing factors. These are identified through discussion and labeled. This is also called a "cause-and-effect" diagram.
3. Discuss possible solutions. Ask a lot of "What if?" questions to examine options. Weigh the pros and cons of alternate approaches.
4. Decide on a solution.

Following a process gives you the advantage of a "pathway" to keep participants on track. If the discussion digresses, you can bring the group back on track by referring to the point in the process. "Whoa," you say, "before we start discussing solutions, are you satisfied we've thoroughly diagnosed the problem?"

If you're going to brainstorm about a topic to come up with ideas and possible actions, here's a process for doing that:

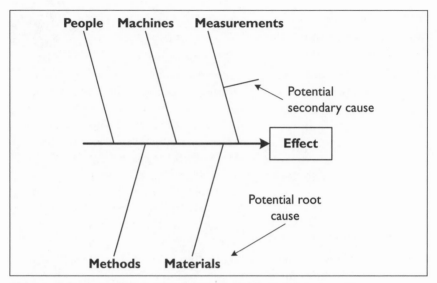

Figure 7-3. A model for a cause-and-effect fishbone diagram

- Spend about 10 minutes collecting ideas.
- The person selected as recorder lists all ideas on flip charts in the speaker's own words.
- No criticisms or judgments about ideas allowed.
- Participants can either take turns giving ideas or call out ideas as they think of them.
- Build on ideas suggested by each other.
- No discussion of ideas during this phase.
- Once the ideas are collected, the group can then start discussing them, with the goal of using the ideas to build a solution or course of action around which the group can find consensus.

Consensus An agreement that everyone willingly accepts. It suggests the general agreement by all group members that a solution or proposal is acceptable enough to support. You build consensus through discussion and modifying ideas to take everyone's thoughts into consideration. Note: majority rule is *not* consensus.

Leadership and Facilitation Skills

In an ideal participative meeting, everyone speaks in turn, clearly articulates their point, offers only relevant information and ideas, and stays focused on the specific subject of discussion. Participants interact tactfully. Agreement is reached. The purpose of the meeting is fully accomplished and everyone goes home happy.

When you lead a participative meeting, your objective is to steer the group toward this ideal. Group dynamics being what they are, you may not achieve "ideal." But you'll get closer to it than what the reality of your meetings may be now. To make the most of participative meetings, follow these steps to facilitate discussions.

Watch the Visual Cues

Be alert to the signals participants send through their body behaviors. Do you notice facial expressions? A person appears to like an idea. Someone else seems bothered by it. Another person looks confused. Are some people shifting in their chairs or glancing at their watches because the discussion's bogged down on an insignificant point?

To be a skillful facilitator, you must be observant. Watch how people react visually and respond accordingly. Help participants express in words what their faces and bodies are communicating.

Remain Neutral—or at Least Objective

The role of the facilitator is to make something easier, in this case a productive discussion. Don't allow your ideas and opinions to inhibit participation. Don't ignore or avoid ideas, opinions, and reactions because you don't agree with them. The participants most likely differ in experience, thinking styles, attitudes, and so forth. Make the most of that diversity. Be willing to open the discussion to all ideas and opinions, whatever you may feel about them personally.

Promote Balanced Participation

If one or two participants monopolize a discussion and others don't speak up at all, you have a meeting that's out of balance. You and the group will miss out on the good ideas passive participants are reluctant to voice. And when a decision is reached, you can't be sure if it's been forced by the more aggressive communicators and whether the more passive really agree or not.

To balance the interaction, draw out those who are slow to speak up. Address them by name. Ask them open questions. Refer to their expertise, not their silence. Say something like "Terry, you've done a lot of work in this area. What are your thoughts about this?"

To balance the discussion, rein in those who monopolize the meeting. Tactfully interrupt: "Marty, before you go on, I'd like to hear some suggestions from others in the group." Then visibly redirect your attention away from the monopolizer and toward other participants.

If a person persists in monopolizing the discussion, take them aside during a break. Tell them you appreciate their interest in the subject and their input shows they want to help get the issue resolved.

> ## Managing Monopolizers
>
> Often, people who regularly monopolize discussions seek attention. You may be able to satisfy their need for attention by assigning them a role. Ask them to record key ideas. Tell them you want them to recap the discussion on a topic. Give them responsibility for getting people back from breaks. Ask them to distribute handouts.

Add, "You know what would really help: if I could hear more from others in the group to make sure I'm getting everyone's point of view." If a monopolizer keeps it up, give them corrective feedback (in private).

Encourage everyone to participate by creating an environment that's conducive to open communication. Voice statements that affirm participants. And refrain from any response (verbal or visual) that could be interpreted as demeaning or derogatory.

Restate Rambling Comments and Questions

Participants sometimes ramble. Some do this when a discussion gets intense and they feel passionate about the subject. Others have so many ideas and issues in mind, they verbalize one, then another, and skip around. And some people simply lack good communication skills.

When you facilitate a meeting, it's essential that you listen attentively, that you help others follow the discussion, and that you keep the discussion focused. You've got the job of making clear the gist of communications. When a participant rambles, do one of two things.

1. *Stop to sort out.* When a speaker starts to switch from one point to another, tactfully interrupt. Say, "Before you go on, I want to be sure I clearly understand your first point." For the benefit of the group, restate it clearly and succinctly.
2. *Recap.* Allow the speaker to continue (provided they're not monopolizing the discussion). When they've finished, sum up what they said. "I heard three concerns expressed in your remarks. First, ..." Count off each point to clarify. Then confirm, "Is that correct?"

Capture Key Points

Someone makes a suggestion. Another participant expresses concern. Someone else raises a question. Two people jump in to answer. Another idea is offered. The discussion becomes *very* participative. You want to be sure key points don't get lost in the process.

To capture key points, use the four P's:

- *Pace.* Moderate the pace of the discussion. If it speeds up to the point where it's difficult to pick out what each participant is saying or the discussion seems to be getting off track, slow it down. Call a time-out. Suggest, "Let's go back to a point Joe made." As you restate the point, speak more slowly and deliberately yourself to set a steadier pace for the group.
- *Probe.* When someone makes a comment and you hear in it a hint of an important point, probe further. "Joe, you were telling us about a customer complaint you received

recently. I had the impression it wasn't the first time this has happened, yes?" (Joe indicates that's right.) You continue, "And these complaints are basically about what?" Use open questions to bring key points to the surface.

- *Poll.* Find out if the group as a whole considers the point important. Ask questions like "How many of you have also run into a problem similar to the one Joe's brought up?" or "How many of you are also concerned about this issue?" Avoid marginalizing participants, making them feel that they're outside the mainstream.

- *Put in writing.* In problem-solving and brainstorming meetings, ask the person in the role of recorder to write down all critical points and key ideas. Use a method that allows for all participants to see them. Use flip chart sheets and tape them up on the walls around the room. Or use an electronic visual board from which you can print copies for everyone. Some facilitators have the recorder use a laptop computer connected to an LCD projector. The drawback to this method is that, for a clearly readable projection, the lights need to be dimmed. Dim lighting tends to drain the energy out of a meeting and makes it more difficult to observe participants' visual cues.

Mediate Differences of Opinion

Take care that discussions don't deteriorate into divisive conflicts. When differences of opinion occur, before participants start taking sides and forming factions, guide the discussion toward resolution. Apply the conflict-facilitation skills outlined in Chapter 6.

Suggest a few moments of silence. Ask participants to use this "quiet time" to:

- make note of their views on the issue.
- sketch a T-chart that lists the pros and cons of each opinion.
- jot down questions that help examine the issue in more depth.

Most important, keep participants focused on the interests and objectives they have in common.

Bringing the Meeting to a Close

At the end of a meeting, briefly address three questions.

1. **What key points did we cover?** Reiterate the points your-self or pose the question to the group. Inviting feedback from participants gives you an indication of how much they gained from the meeting.
2. **What tasks were assigned?** Review tasks that were assigned during the meeting: who's responsible for each task, the date due, and the method of reporting results to participants.
3. **Overall, what did we accomplish?** Echo the purpose of the meeting (which you stated at the outset). In presented meetings, thank people for their time and attention. In participative meetings, thank participants for their contributions to the discussion and commend them on the progress they've made.

Use a Grab Bag Review

TRICKS OF THE TRADE

Here's a fun and effective way to involve participants in doing a review after a mid-meeting break or at the end of a meeting. You'll find it energizes a group and gets people thinking about key points covered.

Use a paper or plastic sack for a Grab Bag. In it, place an assort-ment of items in small plastic baggies. Items might include a variety of nuts and bolts, three or four crayons of different colors, a roll of multi-flavored Life Savers® candies, rubber bands, candy kisses, marbles, or toy action figures.

Ask participants to form into break-out groups of three or four and to name a spokesperson for their group. Have each spokesperson draw from the Grab Bag one item. Give the groups three to five min-utes to discuss how the item they drew symbolizes one key point made in the meeting. Then ask each spokesperson to present their review.

Identify Areas for Improvement

Periodically, ask participants to evaluate the effectiveness of meetings. It's good feedback for you and it gets them thinking about what they might do, too, to make better use of time spent in meetings.

Ask your meeting task force to develop an evaluation form or use one like the sample shown below.

Meeting Evaluation Form	Usually	Sometimes	Rarely
Circle the number of the adverb that most often applies.			
Meetings start on time.	1	2	3
Meetings follow the agenda.	1	2	3
Everyone observes the ground rules.	1	2	3
Everyone comes prepared.	1	2	3
Everyone participates.	1	2	3
Communication is courteous and constructive.	1	2	3
Meetings follow a process for solving problems.	1	2	3
Meetings accomplish the purpose.	1	2	3
Follow-up actions are done and reported on time.	1	2	3
Leadership is effective.	1	2	3
Meetings end on time.	1	2	3

Figure 7-4. A sample form for evaluating the meeting

The Communicator's Checklist for Chapter 7

❑ Determine the cost/benefit factors. They serve as a reminder of the importance of planning and conducting meetings to be effective.

❏ For every meeting, clarify the purpose, develop and distribute a planned agenda, and choose participants and assign roles.

❏ Follow the guidelines for starting on time, staying on track, and closing.

❏ Become a skilled meeting leader and facilitator—and help your employees develop their meeting skills.

Steps to Successful Presentations

Think of all of the ways you communicate: by letters, memos, reports, telephone calls, e-mail, face-to-face conversations, discussions, and presentations. Which gives you the greatest chance to make a powerful impact on people? A skillful presentation.

Every presentation you do is a chance:

- to convey your credibility and competence
- to inform and inspire people
- to persuade others to accept and act on your ideas
- to gain visibility to advance in your career

The French scientist, Louis Pasteur, noted, "Chance favors only the prepared mind." Given what you stand to gain from a good presentation, it pays to be very well prepared.

Prepare a presentation in three stages:

1. Consider the audience.
2. Compose the content.
3. Create enhancements.

Consider the Audience

Memorize this phrase: "It's not about me. It's about *them*." Keep it in mind whenever you develop and deliver a presentation. It helps you focus on *the* most important aspect of any presentation: your audience.

Make Your Message Matter—to Them

Have you ever sat through a presentation and had the impression that the speaker didn't give much thought to you? It's a common audience complaint: "The presenter didn't address *our* needs."

> **Audience** In its broadest sense, anyone and everyone you present to. An audience may be one person or it may consist of ten, hundreds, or thousands of people. Your audience may be employees, peers, your boss, professional colleagues, clients, members of boards, or the general public.

First and foremost, keep in mind the mind-set of your audience. From the moment you begin to prepare a presentation, adopt the point of view of the person or the people you're going to be speaking to. Will you be presenting to your boss? to employees? to peers? View your subject from *their* perspective.

Consider these key questions.

- What do they already know about this subject? What more do they need to know?
- What are their interests and concerns?
- What will speak to them and illuminate their understanding of this topic?
- What will motivate them to act on my message as I want them to?
- What will give them an experience of value in exchange for the time and attention they're going to give me?

The answers to these questions help you determine the content of your presentation and how to communicate it: the level of language to use, the terminology, the references, and the supporting material to include—or exclude.

Compose the Content

What are you going to say when you present? That depends on four factors:

- subject
- audience
- time frame
- setting

Compare two situations.

First situation:
Subject: Your idea for a "change management" team
Audience: Your boss and three top executives
Time: 20 minutes
Setting: Executive board room

Assume that after your presentation they give you the go-ahead to implement your idea. Here's the situation for your next presentation.

Second situation:
Subject: The same: your idea for a "change management" team
Audience: The employees you manage
Time: One hour
Setting: Conference room; casual

Even though the subject is the same, the content of your presentation would be customized to suit the circumstances—audience, time frame, and setting.

Compose the content of a presentation in six steps:

1. objective
2. primary points
3. supporting material
4. transitions
5. recap and close
6. opening and preview

Cut to the Chase

Don't feel compelled to tell people everything you know. Confine the content of your presentation to what they need to know to respond to your presentation in a way that achieves your objective.

Obviously, this order differs from the way you give a presentation. But preparing the content this way speeds and simplifies the process.

Step 1: Establish Your Objective

Your objective expresses what you intend to accomplish by the end of your presentation. State it in "audience action" terms. In other words, what do you want the audience to do as a result of listening to you?

Write it out. State it clearly. And keep it constantly in mind, because your objective governs every part of your presentation. Everything you do—the way you begin, the examples you cite, the visual aids you use—all should be aimed at moving your audience along to satisfy your objective.

Here's a basic format for stating your objective: *When I've finished this presentation, this audience will* _____.

Tailor the basic format to the specific situation. For example, "When I've finished presenting my idea for a change management team, my boss will ..." or "... the employees will ...." Naming the audience serves to remind you to highlight issues of interest to *them*. And it helps you anticipate questions or concerns they may raise.

Step 2: Pick Your Primary Points

Have you ever sat through a presentation and afterwards wondered, "What was that about?" If someone asked what the speaker presented, you'd answer, "A lot of stuff." Another common audience complaint is that the presenter or presentation was "disorganized."

Reality Check

Keep your objective realistic in relation to the audience and time frame. If you attempt to do too much in too little time with an audience that's not yet ready to fully accept what you present, you'll set yourself up for frustration. If you don't achieve your objective, was it because your presentation was lacking? Or because your objective was too lofty?

You may need to do more than one presentation on the subject, with short-term incremental objectives that lead to your overall, end objective.

A speaker can give the impression of being disorganized by shuffling through note papers, showing slides out of order, or just having a disheveled appearance. More often than not, though, it's rambling around a subject that conveys a lack of organization.

A well-organized presentation follows a logical sequence. As you progress from one point to the next, it makes it easier for an audience to listen and absorb the information. And it makes it easier for you to present it.

Begin organizing your presentation by picking the primary points you want to make. These points are to your subject what chapter titles are to a book. They're the main categories under which you group the material you're going to present.

Whenever possible, limit these to not more than three. Think "1-2-3 P's"—the one, two, or three primary points that are essential to your message. Pick points that are:

- most relevant to the audience
- most important for the audience to remember
- pertinent to your objective

On average, people retain only 10% to 20% of what they hear. If your audience remembers little else from your entire presentation, you want them to remember at least these primary points. The reason for limiting primary points to three: our brains tend to store and recall information in pairs and threes.

So far in this chapter, you have an example of picking primary points. This first section is on the subject of preparing a presentation. And the three points are:

1. Consider the audience.
2. Compose the content.
3. Create enhancements.

You'll notice the points are arranged logically, in the order in which they occur. A logical sequence gives the impression of a well-organized presentation.

You can arrange primary points in one of these ways:

Memory Joggers

Tricks of the Trade

Make it easier for people to remember your primary points. Word them using one of the following techniques.

- **Acronym**. Form a word or abbreviation from the first letters of other words. A presentation on customer service, for example, might use the acronym SRV to convey these points: Smile, Respond, Value.
- **Alliteration**. Use words that begin with the same sound. This technique was used in naming the stages to prepare a presentation: Consider, Compose, Create.
- **Basics** (the ABCs or the 3 R's). Management consultant, author, and speaker Kenneth Blanchard used this technique in a presentation on the ABCs of employee performance. His primary points were Attitude, Behavior, and Consequences.
- **Repetition** (of a key word or phrasing). In a presentation intended to impress upon employees the importance of quality, a manager made these primary points: Quality products, Quality service, Quality support.
- **Question format**. Use the words of open questions. A presentation on change management might address these questions: What changes? Who is affected? How do we ease transitions?

- chronologically, by date or in order of occurrence
- spatially or geographically
- by priority, building from least to most important

Step 3: Select Supporting Material

Primary points are like headlines in your presentation. They don't stand on their own. You need to clarify, explain, describe, or substantiate each point with supporting material.

Supporting material includes:

- examples
- analogies, comparisons, or contrasts
- quotations
- statistical data
- results of surveys, tests, or research
- stories
- audiovisual aids, including graphs, charts, models, props, photos, and illustrations

Select supporting material that is:

• suited to the subject
• consistent with your objective
• appropriate to the audience

Do you recall the communication profiles described in Chapter 3? Knowing which profiles are in your audience helps you select the type of material to use. If you're going to present to an audience of predominantly concrete thinkers, your presentation will be more convincing if you use objective, qualitative material. On the other hand, conceptual thinkers will respond better to more subjective, qualitative material. In many situations, an audience is mixed and you'll get the best results using a mix of supporting material.

How much supporting material should you use? Enough to establish the primary point, but not so much that you overdo it. Refrain from giving so many examples, telling so many stories, and citing so many statistics that you bore the audience to tears.

> ### Appeal to the Audience
>
> It's human nature. We tend to select material that appeals to us or that's easily available. Remember: it's not about *me*, it's about *them*—people in the audience on the receiving end of your presentation. Know their profiles and preferences, and use the type of material most likely to make the greatest impact on them.

Select material based on four criteria:

• It clearly illustrates the primary point.
• It supports your objective.
• You can communicate it concisely.
• The sum of all your material is doable within the time allotted to your presentation.

Some presenters try to pack too much material into a limited time frame. Others ad-lib more than necessary. Some presentations are interrupted and slowed by questions and comments from the audience. And too many presenters neglect to do a timed run-through of the presentation beforehand.

Identify in advance material you can omit if you find you're running short of time when you present. It happens all the time. Guard against running over your allotted time, because audiences don't like it.

Step 4: Use Transitions

Transitions bridge from one primary point to the next. In one sentence, you restate the point you're leaving and introduce the point you're going to. It sounds like this: "Now that you know the steps to compose the content, let's consider the kind of enhancements you want to create." Because transitions link points, they add a sense of sequence to your presentation.

Because they're such tiny pieces of a presentation, transitions are often overlooked. But without them a presentation can seem disorganized. According to Roger Axtell, author of *Do's and Taboos of Public Speaking,* "On average, people listen for only three seconds out of every 10." Suppose if, during those seven seconds when some people aren't listening, you go from one point to the next without voicing a transition. When the people who tuned out tune in again, you're talking about something else. To them, your presentation sounds disjointed or they get the impression you're rambling.

Pause before stating a transition. Modulate your voice when you say it. A vocal variation alerts the audience that something different is about to happen and it tends to "awaken" those who have temporarily tuned out.

Step 5: Recap and Close

The recap is easy to compose. It's a simple summary statement of your primary points. Using the earlier example of a presentation on change management, the recap might be worded, "You've heard what changes we expect, who will be affected, and how a change management team will ease the process."

Composing the close takes a bit more thought. It's the "finale" that should always:

- impress upon the audience a significant point
- end on a positive note

- conclude the presentation decisively

Don't ramble on aimlessly and endlessly, sounding uncertain about how to wrap it up. End strong!

There are many ways to close a presentation. You can end with a rhetorical question, a quotation, a striking statistic, a humorous anecdote, a moving story, and/or a statement that echoes your objective.

Statements related to your objective do one of the following things.

- **Reflect.** Reiterate the objective and ask the audience to reflect on what they've heard.
- **Direct.** Instruct the audience to do something by way of applying what they've heard.
- **Decide.** Ask the audience to make a decision: approve your proposal, fund your project, buy your product.

Step 6: Open and Preview

Does this situation sound familiar to you? You have a presentation to give on Thursday morning. Wednesday night, working late at home, you're seated at the dining room table with a blank tablet in front of you or at the computer staring at a blank screen. You start to compose the opening: "Good morning. I'll be talking about ..." Nah, no good. You start over. After half a dozen or so false starts, you begin to dread this presentation.

> **TRICKS OF THE TRADE**
> **What About Q&A?**
> If you set aside time at the end for a question-and-answer period, invite questions after the recap but before the actual close. Never put a Q&A session last. If you do, you run the risk of getting a tough or negative question that ends your presentation on a sour note. Keep control of the close so you can wrap up your presentation as you prefer.

How does that compare with what we've done so far? If you've followed along from the beginning of this chapter, you've already composed the objective (easy to do), picked your primary points (easy to do), selected supporting material (takes a bit more effort), jotted down transitions (very easy to do), and decided how to close. All the while, your brain has been processing ideas and information about the subject. By the time you get to composing the opening last, it'll come more naturally and easily to you.

How you open is one of the most important aspects of a presentation. You have seconds in which to capture the interest and attention of your listeners. You can't do that with an ordinary ho-hum opening. You need an opening that's fresh and creative.

Open with one (or a combination) of the following techniques.

- Compelling quote
- Striking statistic
- Rhetorical question
- Humorous anecdote
- Engaging story
- Visual aid

Given the importance of the opening, know it cold. For some presentations, you may not have much lead time to prepare. But do prepare and prac-

> **⚠ CAUTION!**
>
> ### Never Open with a Joke
>
> You've heard it. The presenter who opens with a joke that's so stale it's not funny. The manager who has no sense of comedic timing or botches the punch line. The speaker who carelessly tells a joke that's offensive to someone in the audience. You have more to lose and less to gain by opening with a joke. So don't.

tice your opening. Prepare *what* you're going to say; practice *how* you're going to say it. How you deliver the opening sets the stage.

Immediately, even before you begin to speak, people start to form perceptions. From the outset, you want your audience to perceive that you're confident, knowledgeable about the subject, and interested in them. You want them to perceive that what follows the opening is worth tuning in to. So the opening needs to be engaging.

There's an added advantage to knowing your opening well. Most people who feel nervous about presenting find the "butterflies in the stomach" start to flutter during the first few minutes of a presentation. "Once I get past the beginning," they say, "I'm OK." Being well prepared to deliver a dynamic opening gets you through those tense moments with ease.

From the opening, transition into your presentation with a preview. Like the recap you do at the end, the preview is a brief statement of your one, two, or three primary points. It serves to let the audience know what to expect.

The Path of a Presentation

Once you've composed the content, lay it out as shown in Figure 8-1.

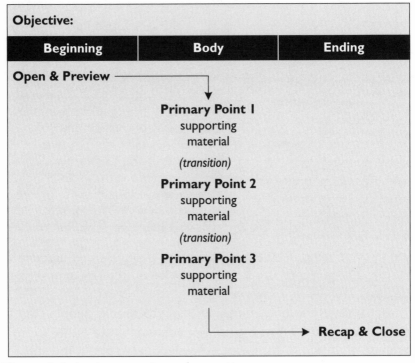

Figure 8-1. Laying out the presentation

Review your presentation to ensure that, from opening to close, it flows. See that it progresses smoothly and sequentially, one point logically leading to the next. View it from the standpoint of the audience. If you (as a member of the audience) were listening to this, would it keep your attention? Would the material appeal to you (an employee, the boss, your peers)?

Does it make sense? And check that each part serves to support your objective.

Create Enhancements

Once the content is composed, you're ready to create material to enhance your presentation, namely:

- visual aids
- handouts

Both are forms of support. They should be designed and used to add interest and impact. They should never detract from your message or from your presence as the presenter.

Three T's

A long-standing approach to presenting suggests:
- In the beginning, preview: Tell 'em what you're going to tell 'em.
- In the body: Tell them.
- At the end, recap: Tell 'em what you told 'em.

If this strikes you as redundant, bear in mind: people don't listen constantly. Periodically, they tune out and miss some points. Add to that the massive amounts of information we're exposed to every day. We don't assimilate all of it. We remember best what we hear repeatedly. So repeat your primary points three times: in the preview, in the body, and in the recap.

As with everything else in an effective presentation, visual aids and handouts are intended for the benefit of the audience. Use what helps the audience listen, follow along, understand, learn, and remember.

Never use visual aids or handouts as a crutch to help you present. Know your subject well enough that you don't need a crutch. And don't use visual aids merely to "wow 'em!" with special effects. Doing so can dilute the impact of your message. What will people remember afterwards? Not what you said, but the visual effects they saw.

Visual Aids

With advancements in technology, many people have become enamored of multimedia and computer-generated slide presentations. While high-tech tools for visual aids have their place, they're not always the best choice for all presentations.

Choose the type of visual aid best suited to the situation. Consider:

How Cute!

During a presentation to prospective buyers, a vendor used a computer-generated slide show. Whenever he paused the slide show to speak to the group, an animated image of a puppy running through a maze appeared on the screen behind him. What did people in the audience discuss afterwards? Not the vendor's products, pricing, or customer service. They were enthralled by that cute puppy.

He learned a useful lesson from the experience. Always blank the screen when you're finished showing a visual aid. If an image remains on the screen, it distracts the audience and they may miss an important point that follows.

- the size of the audience
- the setting and lighting
- your budget for the presentation
- access to equipment and your ability to operate it proficiently
- how much lead time you have to prepare visual aids
- the length and nature of the presentation

For a 10-minute message presented to a large audience, a slide show or multimedia presentation might be best. For a one-hour interactive presentation to a small group, a low-tech flip chart, visual board, or overhead transparencies could be most effective.

To enhance a presentation, visual aids (whichever form you use) should be:

- Clear
- Colorful
- Pictorial
- On occasion, surprisingly or humorously creative

Clear. Check that every visual aid is clearly readable by people seated the greatest distance away or at the far sides of the room. If you write on flip charts, a visual board, or blank overhead transparencies, write large and legibly.

For printed visuals, use large fonts: a sans-serif style for a single-line headline (which may be in ALL CAPS), a traditional serif style for the body (in upper- and lower- case type). Limit the lines of text to not more than six per slide. Summarize with bullet points. Leave space between the lines and at the margins for clarity and eye relief.

If you must use italic type, use it sparingly. Don't underline words; use bold type instead. Never use a multilevel outline format.

Never copy a page of printed material onto a visual aid and read from it. Most people in an audience perceive that as a lack of presentation skill on your part and a waste of their time. (They could read it themselves.) If the audience must have all of the information on a page, give it to them in a handout.

Colorful. Color enhances interest and improves retention. Use colors consistent with the point the visual aid illustrates or the emotion it's meant to elicit. For example: green is a "cool" color; it signifies growth, income, creativity. Red is a "hot" color; it suggests debt, expenses, anger, passion. Dark colors convey a professional or serious intent. Light, bright colors are more fun and friendly.

Limit colors to two, not more than three on each visual. For more effects, use various shades of intensity. With adjacent colors, be sure there's sufficient contrast for viewers to clearly distinguish between them. For contrast and clarity, use dark colors against a light background for titles and captions (or vice versa).

Pictorial. Long after people have forgotten words, they'll remember an image. Visual aids should be just that—visual. Charts and graphs are visual; pictographs are more so. Slides that display only lines of text are more verbal than visual. They're called visual aids because the audience can see them and they help to focus attention or emphasize a point. But to be truly visual and therefore more effective, add a familiar symbol or an appropriate clip art image.

Creative. With the millions of meetings and presentations that go on every day, we're used to the usual visual aids, even the high-tech types. Special effects have little effect; we've seen them all before. And the longer a presentation goes on, the more important it is for you to be creative. Creativity stimulates curiosity, heightens interest, and arouses the attentiveness of that person who's slumping in their chair and nodding off after 20 minutes.

Unless you happen to work in a creative profession like advertising, it's unlikely every visual aid you use will be creative. But once in a while, insert one that is. Don't resort to gimmicks. Be inventive. When you're creating visual aids, ask yourself, What's an original way to illustrate or demonstrate this point? What object can I use as a prop to get my point across? How can I involve the audience in some short activity so they see the meaning in my message?

Handouts

People like handouts. A handout gives them something to take notes on. They can refer to it later. And they feel like they're getting something for free.

Prepare handouts that correspond to and reinforce your message.

- Organize the handout so it follows the sequence of your presentation.
- Every page should be clean and readable. Don't use copies of illegible copies.
- For multipage handouts, include a table of contents.
- In the top margin of every page, print the subject at the left and the page number in the upper right corner. For date-sensitive material, add the date of the presentation.
- Use signposts. When you present a point that's in a handout, direct the audience to where it can be found: "Turn to page 3 where you'll see item number 6 ...." If you don't signpost, some people flip through the pages of a handout trying to find what you're talking about. Signposting also conditions the audience to stay with you so they don't look ahead in the handout. (And if they do, so what?)

In some situations, you may have a report or proposal you'd prefer to give the audience after your presentation. In that case, give as a handout a one- or two-page executive summary: an outline of your presentation that highlights your primary points. Let people know they'll be getting the detailed documentation after the presentation.

Automatic Handouts

Do you use a presentation software program to prepare slides or overhead transparencies? The popular programs also have an option to print handouts. Choose the option that prints two or three slide images on the left half of the page and adds lines to the right of the slides. Handouts in this format make it easy for an audience to follow along when you display the visual aids, and people like the lines for taking notes.

Between Preparation and Presentation—Practice

You're prepared. You've considered the audience, composed the content, and created visual aids and handouts. You're ready to present—if you know your subject very well, if you're confident in front of a group, and if you're sure you can complete your presentation in the time allotted to it. Otherwise, practice your presentation.

Do a timed run-through. If it's a high-stakes presentation (you have a lot at stake) or part of a team presentation, rehearse it in a simulated situation. Ask a few people to sit in on your practice sessions to observe and offer constructive feedback. If a presentation is so high-stakes that your success depends on the outcome, get a coach to audit it and give you suggestions for improvement.

Communicate Skillfully

You're sitting across the desk from your boss ready to present your idea. In a management meeting with your peers, you're about to present your department's results. In the conference room, you're going to present to employees at the weekly staff meeting.

Every presentation boils down to this. The content and visual aids and handouts you've prepared amount to nothing more than words on paper—until you communicate them. During a presentation, everything you've learned about communicating effectively comes into play.

Capture and Keep Attention

Think of presenting as a competitive sport. What are you competing for? Attention. Just because people attend a presentation doesn't mean they're attentive to it. You need to captivate and keep their interest.

Now more than ever before that's not an easy thing to do. We're bombarded by information. Our attention span is short. And it's shrinking due to the quickening pace of our lives, the influence of the media, and 20-second sound bites. Computer functions are speeding up; software engineers and Web-page designers aim for getting a program up within five to seven seconds. Watching TV, we instantaneously click the remote control and switch to another channel if the one we're watching doesn't keep our interest. We're accustomed to it: get information quickly, in small doses, and move on. Bear these factors in mind when you present.

Start with a strong opening. Move quickly into the "meat" of your message. (Don't risk losing people by dwelling too long on the opening.) Then, throughout your presentation, watch the timing and tempo.

Don't belabor any one point. After two or three minutes, give the audience a "change of pace." You might, for example, comment on a point. Then display a visual aid to further explain or emphasize the point. Elicit a response from the audience. Quicken the pace of your delivery or slow it down. Inject humor. Even as you maintain the continuity of your message, you need to vary your manner of delivery to sustain the interest of the audience.

Verbal, Vocal, and Visual Cues

Review Chapter 2. Everything it describes about verbal, vocal, and visual cues applies to a presentation—and more so. In conversations and discussions, cues are picked up by one person or a few. In a presentation to a group, all (or most) eyes and ears are on you. Your cues, or the lack of them, are picked up by everyone in the audience.

In most presentations, unlike conversations, people don't interrupt to ask, "What do you mean?" You need to make your meaning clear.

Verbal. Use words that accurately state the points you make. Use short sentences. Periodically pause to let listeners catch up with what you're saying and mull it over for a moment. Refrain from jargon or weighty words that might interfere with the audience understanding.

Vocal. Speak up and speak clearly. Develop

> **Censor Yourself**
>
> Be sensitive to the diversity of most audiences. Be aware that some differences aren't visible, but have to do with people's inner beliefs. Strip out of your presentation any remarks that smack of bias. Don't tell off-color jokes or unseemly stories. Don't use humor that may offend someone.

resonance in your voice so it projects well. Use vocal inflections to add meaning to your message. Vary the pitch, rate, volume, and tone. Vocal variations help to sustain the interest of an audience.

Some people adopt a different persona when they present. They feel they have to "perform" and sound "official." You don't. Refrain from talking *at* people. Speak naturally, as though you're conversing with the audience. In most situations, a conversational style has a more positive effect. It puts people at ease—the audience and you.

Visual. Express your message through facial expressions, gestures, and movement. An expressive and energetic style enlivens an audience and keeps people tuned in to you. Of course, if the subject is very serious and the setting somber, you'd tone it down.

If the setting allows for it, move to different spots around the front of the room or on the platform. If it's appropriate to the situation, move into and among people in the audience; doing so creates a sense of connection between them and you. It also makes them move to keep their eyes on you, which helps people stay alert.

Visually, one of the most effective things you can do is make and maintain eye contact with the audience. If you must refer to notes, know your material well enough that you only need to glance at key word notes on occasion. If you keep your head down, buried in notes, the audiences misses your visual expressiveness—and you miss spotting their reactions.

Throughout a presentation, you're communicating cues. So is the audience. In some presentations, people voice feedback in the form of questions and comments. In all presentations, they're giving you feedback via nonverbal cues. Watch for them. And adjust your presentation accordingly.

If the audience appears nonresponsive, it may be a sign they've grown disinterested. Change the tempo; pick up the pace; do something different. If, after making a point, you notice expressions that convey confusion, clarify the point. Add an example, give a comparison, or sketch a visual aid. On the other hand, once people nod ("yes") and appear to understand and agree, move on to the next point.

How to Handle Questions

A common concern before giving a presentation is "What if someone asks me a question?" Welcome questions. See them as positive cues. They indicate people are awake and paying attention. And most questions signal an interest in the subject

Be prepared to answer questions. When you're composing the content of your presentation, consider the kinds of questions people are likely to ask. Depending on the subject, you can expect an audience will want answers to at least these three questions.

- How much does it cost?
- How long will it take?
- How will it affect me?

When you review the material you're going to present, you may come up with other probable questions as well. Anticipating the questions that people are likely to ask, prepare to answer them. Then you have two options.

- Incorporate the answers into the content you prepare. At the appropriate point, say something like "I expect you want to know the impact this will have on the department" or "You probably want to know how long this will take." Then give the answer.
- Wait until the presentation to see if you're asked the question or not. If you are, having anticipated it, you're ready with an answer.

When you're asked a question, always follow these three steps:

1. Focus your full attention on the person asking the question. Look at them. Listen attentively. If the question isn't clear or if you need to "buy time" to formulate an answer, paraphrase the question.
2. Acknowledge the person. Say, "That's a good question" or "I'm glad you brought that up" or "You've raised an interesting point." Affirmations like these signal others in the group that you're responsive to the audience and receptive to their questions.
3. Answer the question. When you answer, address the group as a whole.

To a direct question, give a direct answer. Question: "You're asking us to work extra hours while we convert to this new system. Will we get overtime pay?" Answer: "Yes" or "No." If people want to know more, they'll ask more. Don't dig yourself into a hole or take up time unnecessarily by giving a lengthy answer to a simple, straightforward question.

For a detailed question, apply the "three P's." Answer with one, two, or three primary points. Offer an example by way of explanation.

Three Don'ts When Dealing with Questions

Here are three things you never want to do when responding to questions:

- Don't *Defend.* A defensive reaction pits you against the person who asked the question. In the presence of everyone attending your presentation, you'll come off looking bad if you get defensive.
- Don't *Debate.* Someone asks a question. You answer. They get argumentative. Debating will derail your presentation. Defer the discussion until later. Suggest, "I appreciate your concern. And I'll be glad to discuss it with you when we're finished here."
- Don't *Disparage.* A question that may strike you as silly could be an important issue to the person who asked. Never react to a question with a belittling remark like "We don't have time for irrelevant questions" or "Why would you ask a question like *that?*" (implying that you think it's a stupid question).

If you're asked a question you don't know the answer to, respond in one of three ways.

- Say something like "That's a good question. I wish I had a good answer for it, but I don't. I'll look it up and get back to you." (Then do so.)
- Refer the question to the audience. Addressing the group as a whole, ask, "Who has some experience with that?" or "What are your thoughts about Terry's question?"
- Give the question back to the person who asked it (if doing so is appropriate to the situation). "You've raised an interesting point. Why don't you look that up and let us know what you find out?" If you have an employee who asks questions to "test" you, this response will soon put a stop to it.

Keeping Calm

Do you get nervous about presenting? Many people do. And it's evident to an audience. A quaking voice, shrill pitch, rapid rate of speech, wooden posture, reluctance to make eye contact—all such cues convey anxiety. An audience sees that as a lack of

confidence or uncertainty about your subject.
Nervousness is rooted in one of these reasons:

- **Unprepared**. Don't try to "wing it." Knowing what you stand to gain from giving a good presentation (and what you stand to lose if you give a poor one), prepare. The better prepared and practiced you are, the more confident you'll be. And confidence combats anxiety.
- **Self-conscious**. Assuming you're well prepared, you may be nervous because you feel self-conscious. Here's another good reason to focus on the audience. When you do, it takes your focus off of you. The more audience-conscious you are, the less self-conscious you'll be. Concentrate on giving the audience a good experience when you present, and it'll be a better experience for you, too.
- **Little experience**. As with almost everything, the more experience you gain, the less nervous you'll be. Effective presentations are such an asset that it's to your advantage to sharpen your skills. Take training. Get practice through involvement in a group like Toastmasters International. And seek opportunities to present, improving your skills and becoming more self-assured each time you do.

The Communicator's Checklist for Chapter 8

❑ Focus on the audience. Know their communication profiles, preferences, and perspectives. Make your message meaningful to them.

❑ Always be well prepared before you present.

❑ Capture and keep the attention and interest of people in your audience.

❑ Present with energy and expressive verbal, vocal, and visual cues.

❑ Be ready for questions—and welcome them.

E-Communications

W hat does the "e" in e-communications stand for? *Electronic*, of course. It might also stand for *easy, efficient, expedited*. Used properly, it can mean *effective*. And beware: it could mean *exposure* to legal liability for the organization.

Technology has expanded our access and ability to communicate with just about anyone, anywhere, at any time. Electronic, computerized systems have added speed, simplicity, and economy to written and voice communication.

E-communication has also been the subject of complaints. You may have thought or voiced a few yourself. "It takes hours to go through all of my e-mail." "That voice-mail system has more menu options than my favorite restaurant."

No form of communication—interpersonal or electronic—is flawless. But with e-communication, you can improve the exchange by following a few simple guidelines. For our purposes, we'll look at e-mail, voice mail, and fax in a business context.

What's Best?

Choose the medium best suited to the message and the circumstances. Don't automatically do what's most convenient for you at the moment or what you happen to prefer. For the best results when dealing with people, consider these factors.

What Does the Recipient Prefer?

With most of the clients I work with, we exchange messages via e-mail. So during a telephone call with a new client, I asked for her e-mail address. "Oh, that," she said with a tone of voice that suggested she wasn't a fan. I took it as a cue and asked, "How would you like me to stay in touch with you?" By phone, she said, or fax for sending documents. As we worked together and I got to know her better, I noticed she had excellent interpersonal skills. She favors building bridges of relationship—person to person. The moral to the story is: be flexible to adapt.

In 1998, the American Management Association surveyed human resource executives. Of the means of communication used most often, e-mail ranked highest at 36% and the telephone came in second at 26%. But more than a third of the respondents said they prefer face-to-face meetings.

Unfortunately, we don't always have the luxury of time or proximity to talk with someone in person. Sometimes the information we need to convey doesn't call for a face-to-face conversation. Which brings us to the next question.

What's the Nature of the Communication?

Do you need to notify all employees of an upcoming meeting? Report on midyear results to your boss? Give a team leader directions on how to proceed with the next phase of a complex project? Cancel today's luncheon meeting with a colleague across town?

In the first situation, an e-mail will do. In others, you'll find it more effective to meet in person so you can offer explanations and assess the other person's response. In the last occurrence, leaving a voice-mail message or paging the person would be the best option.

What Will Get a Timely Response?

Be attuned to how quickly people respond to various media (which is often related to their personal preference). Some people check their e-mail numerous times throughout the day and reply to every message immediately. Others don't.

In organizations where e-mail has become the norm and employees often use it for fun, a serious request related to business may get no more attention (maybe less) than the latest round of e-mail jokes. When a deadline is looming, you may have to pick up the phone and/or fax an *urgent* request.

Is It Confidential?

If your message contains material of a confidential or sensitive nature, take care to use a medium that ensures it'll remain between you and the recipient.

Public or Private? Before you forward or post an e-mail message, ask the sender's permission. If you print e-mail messages on a shared printer, be aware: anyone might read them.

It's happened. A manager e-mails a confidential message to an employee. A coworker is using the employee's computer and, on a whim, peeks at the e-mail messages. Oops.

Five Fundamental Factors

Communication of any kind is most effective when it takes into account the answers to questions in five categories: who, what, when, where, and why.

1. **Who.** Who are you communicating to? Within or outside the organization, what's their position relative to yours? Based on who's going to receive your message, what impression do you want it to make?
2. **What.** What's the subject of your message? What points do you need to cover? What style and tone are appropriate?
3. **When.** If you're writing or calling about an event (e.g., an appointment, meeting, deadline), when is it? When do you need a reply? If you've asked the recipient to contact you in person (or if they want to), when is the best time for them to reach you?
4. **Where.** Where is the event? Where does the recipient contact you to reply?

5. Why. Why are you communicating this? What's the purpose of your message? What do you hope to accomplish with it?

Answering the "why?" question is especially pertinent to using e-mail in business. Some users find e-mail so quick and easy that they give little thought to what they send or who they send it to. A story one user finds amusing gets forwarded to someone else, who then forwards it to an entire address book or contacts list. Why?

Imagine if every time you retrieved your e-mail messages, they spilled out onto your desktop—literally. No matter how it comes, few of us have little time and less patience for heaps of unnecessary mail. If you don't want to be inundated with "stuff," it stands to reason neither do other people. So before you take up your time and theirs, consider the question: "Why is this message necessary?" In business, consider this companion question: "Does this belong on the organization's communications network?"

E-Mail

You're at your desk in the office. You've got your thinking cap on; your mind's on business. You're awaiting a reply to an important message you sent yesterday. You check your e-mail. Several items appear in the in-box. On the subject line, one shows URGENT!!! You click on it and read:

> hey yo—gotta get docs to doofus asap :-< do u hv final figs fer me? b glad when this prjcts over—sick of it!!! u gonna b @ TGIF bash? shd b a blast!!! heard Suzie Q ..... dont say u heard it fm me—ciao
>
> K

If you haven't ever seen this kind of message, you're among a fortunate few.

In the past, there was a clear distinction between business and personal communications. Interoffice memos and correspondence on company letterhead were different from personal notes, both in appearance and in the style of writing.

Eliminate Emoticons

What do you think when you see this? :-) or :-|| or :-\ BTW, FWIW, GMTA, IMHO

If you use e-mail acronyms and symbols, are you certain the reader will interpret them accurately? If not, don't use them. When in doubt, spell it out.

You may be savvy about these symbols, called *smileys* or emoticons (icons that signify emotions). Not all businesspeople are. Some see them as a form of slang that's inappropriate in business communications. Others, intent on business, find emoticons distracting.

That's not the case with e-mail. Some people use it as often, sometimes more, for personal messaging. As a result, the line between personal and business communication has blurred. Some users write and send e-mails to the boss, a customer, or all employees as casually (and sometimes carelessly) as they do e-mails to their bosom buddies. The informality has created some problems.

For the sake of clarity and your credibility, follow these guidelines when using e-mail for business communications.

Write for the Reader

With e-mail, or any form of written communication, readability is key.

You can zap a message instantaneously across cyberspace, print it on embossed letterhead, or scroll it across the heavens with a skywriting plane. No matter how you send a message, if it lacks readability, the recipient won't read it all the way through. If it does get read, it won't create the positive impression you want to convey.

Write with the reader in mind. Consider their perspective. Write to their level of comprehension. Use techniques for the reader's convenience. And recognize that, like you, your readers are busy people. So KISS the message: Keep It Short and Straightforward.

In the Beginning

You begin by keying on the "To" line a name or e-mail address. You may add names to the "cc" (carbon copy) and "bcc" (blind carbon copy) lines. (The difference between the two "copy" lines is that "bcc" recipients are not revealed in the message to your "To" or "cc" recipients.) Double-check these entries before you press "Send." Watch that you don't inadvertently send a message to someone it's not intended for.

If you send e-mails to a contacts list or address book, keep your list current. If you have occasion to e-mail confidential material, be doubly careful. Does your organization have a policy that restricts distribution of confidential items? Make sure everyone you send such information to is authorized to receive it.

Next comes the "Subject" line. Like the headline of a newspaper column, it should convey the theme or key point of the message and capture the reader's attention. When sending a message to multiple recipients, make the subject line generic enough to appeal to all readers.

Indicate if a message is a priority. Reserve "Top Priority" or "Urgent" headings for messages that truly are. Use such designations sparingly. If you label most of your e-mails "Urgent," you'll get a reputation like the legendary boy who cried wolf. When you send a message that really is urgent, recipients won't take seriously the "Urgent" heading. Or you'll be perceived as a manager who's constantly in crisis. (Even if you are, you don't want others to form that perception of you.)

Omit formal salutations, like "Dear ...." It is courteous, though, to start a message with the recipient's name. Address the person as you would if you were speaking to them in person.

The Body of Your Message

Limit each e-mail message to one subject. Here's why.

Suppose you have three subjects to cover with one person.

1. *Your subject*: notify the person of an upcoming meeting.
   Their action: reply to you immediately.
2. *Your subject*: ask about the status of a contract.
   Their action: forward the message to another person who has the information.
3. *Your subject*: answer a policy question the person had.
   Their action: print a copy of the message to keep on file.

If you combine all three subjects in the same message, you make it more cumbersome for the recipient to separate them out for different actions. When you put each subject in a separate message, it's easier for the recipient to respond. And the replies you receive are each confined to one subject, making it quicker and easier for you to read through them.

When composing e-mails, use a "top-down" approach. We tend to remember best what we read first and last. So put the most important point in the first paragraph. In the paragraphs that follow, add detail in descending order of importance. At the end, echo the most important point you began with by briefly restating it.

When you ask a recipient to take some action:

- if the message is short enough to fit on one screen, state what you need at the end.
- with longer messages, state what you need at the beginning.

Get to the point. Readers want to get to the gist of a message on the first screen. Preferably, the reader won't have to scroll down more than a second screen. For messages longer than two screens, consider using an attachment.

If you refer to days or time frames, be specific. You know what you mean by "Monday" or "next month," but don't assume the recipient does. Which Monday? Add the date: "Monday, 4/25." By "next month" do you mean the new month that starts tomorrow or the month that's next after that? Spell it out so there's no doubt.

Keep your communication constructive. Don't put in a business e-mail what you wouldn't write in a letter that went into company files. (In some cases, e-mail messages are retained on an organization's computer files.) Don't put in an e-mail what you wouldn't say in person. Never e-mail material that's inappropriate in the workplace.

At the End

Omit formal closings like "Sincerely yours." End your message in a courteous manner, using a closing like "Regards" or "Thanks" or "See you soon."

Make it easy for read-ers to respond to you. Traditional memo forms and letterhead are imprint-ed with information that lets the reader know how to contact you. The only contact information evi-

Douse the Flames

In e-mail jargon, a "flame" is an inflammatory message. Some users view e-mail as an ideal vehicle to vent. Don't. Ask employees to refrain from firing off messages in anger. Flaming fuels hostilities and stirs up conflicts.

dent on an e-mail is your e-mail address. What if the recipient wants to call you? Or send you an overnight express delivery? Or put material in the mail to you?

When you send an e-mail message to someone who may not know how to get in touch with you, add contact information at the end. Include your telephone number, extension, fax number, and address. List your street address; express services don't deliver to P.O. boxes. E-mail programs make it easy to create and use "signature" files that automatically add contact informa-tion to your messages.

Formatting

As rushed as most busi-nesspeople are these days, few read any type of corre-spondence word for word and line for line. Most of us scan the text. Format your messages to make it easy for the reader to quickly pick out important points.

Before You Press "Send"

Once sent, an e-mail message can't be taken back. You may think a message is clever, comical, or cute. What will the recipient think? Will they find it a waste of time? Will they see it as biased or offensive? Consider the recipient's likely reaction before you click on "Send."

- Keep paragraphs short. Is a one-sentence paragraph acceptable? Absolutely.
- Use double-line spacing between paragraphs. Without this visible separation, it's more difficult for readers to distinguish between the different points in your message. The added blank space between paragraphs also pro-vides relief from eyestrain.

- Use bullets to set apart key points.
- Use upper- and lowercase characters, as you would writing a traditional letter. If typing skill is not your strong suit, you may feel this slows you down. But it makes text easier to read.
- Refrain from using ALL CAPS. TEXT WRITTEN IN ALL CAPS IS MORE DIFFICULT TO READ. IT ALSO GIVES THE IMPRESSION THAT THE LETTERS ARE SCREAMING OFF THE SCREEN! THE READER WONDERS, WHY ARE YOU SHOUTING AT ME!?
- don't use all lowercase type. it slows reading. separate sentences have the appearance of running together. that makes reading more difficult. it can also suggest carelessness (or laziness) on your part.
- Limit the use of **bold type**, *italic type*, and underlining, or don't use them at all. If you overuse special effects, they become less special: they clutter your writing and interfere with its clarity. And some effects don't carry across on all systems.
- Use a clean, traditional typeface like Times Roman or Helvetica. Readability improves with a typeface that recipients are familiar with from newspapers and magazines. If you like fancy typefaces, save them for personal messages.
- Use a type size not less than 10 point, preferably 12. E-mail messages are read off computer screens in all kinds of lighting conditions. Type that's too small makes reading difficult. Type that's too large takes up too much space.
- Use a line length between 40 and 60 characters. Readers can more quickly scan shorter line lengths. Because the reader's eye has less distance to travel from left margin to right, shorter lines also cause less eye fatigue, a factor when reading off a computer screen.
- When a message fills two or more screens, include a table of contents if it's applicable to your subject. Put it at the top, after the opening line. To conserve space, list your contents horizontally rather than vertically. For example:

"Here's the summary you asked for, outlined in three parts: 1. Concept, 2. Phases, 3. Budget"

Number the points that follow in the text. A table of contents and numbered items are a convenience for the reader, who can quickly spot each item as they scroll down the screen.

Attachments

You open an e-mail message and find it runs on and on. As you scroll from one screen to another and another, your cell phone rings, your pager vibrates—and this message never seems to come to an end.

Instead of sending lengthy, multi-screen messages, use the "Attachment" feature. You can also use it to transmit documents with special formatting or graphics you may not be able to create in the e-mail program itself.

When you attach a document, your e-mail message serves as an "executive summary." Don't repeat in the e-mail message what appears in the attachment, or vice versa.

In the message, briefly describe what's attached. Give attachments descriptive filenames. If you attach more than one file, don't label them doc1, doc2, doc3. Use filenames that let the recipient know what each document is.

Style and Tone

In recent years, the style of writing has relaxed, even in traditional business documents. You've probably noticed it in business publications, newspapers, books, and better-written business letters.

Gone are the "old rules" that said you shouldn't start a sentence with a conjunction (and,

A Question of Compatibility

Have you ever received an attachment you couldn't open on your computer? It's time-consuming and frustrating. Before you add an attachment to an e-mail message, check with the recipient to find out if they'll be able to open it. Or send a short test file. If your computer has the capability to save documents in different file formats, ask the recipient which format they prefer.

but, or). Yes, you can. Or you shouldn't end a sentence with a preposition (words like *of, for, from, before, around, about, through*). Yes, you can and should if it makes the message easier to read.

Readers respond best to writing that reflects a conversational style. In e-mail messages, where the approach is typically less formal than in other types of business writing, a conversational style is not only acceptable. It's expected. It's the norm.

> **Key Term**
>
> **Conversational style**
> When read aloud, a conversational style of writing sounds like the writer's talking to you. The tone is congenial; the text more readable. The writing flows naturally. It's a personable approach to written communications.

You can develop a conversational style, and improve your writing overall, with a few simple techniques.

- Write in the active voice. Notice the difference between these two sentences.

  Active: You can use e-mail to notify employees of upcoming meetings.

  Passive: Alerting employees to upcoming meetings can be done using e-mail.

  The active voice places the subject of the sentence—the doer of the action—first. It adds liveliness to your writing and sounds less bureaucratic. It also makes it clear who's doing the action.

- Use action verbs that add strength to a statement. Compare these examples.

  So-so: Let's have a discussion of the matter.

  Stronger: Let's discuss the matter.

  The verb "discuss" replaces the noun "discussion."

  So-so: The team is lacking a strategy.

  Stronger: The team lacks a strategy.

  Changing verbs ending in "ing" makes your writing more compact and direct.

- Use contractions.

  Does anyone talk like this?

  "If you are going to be in town, let us meet Monday morning. I would not ask you to take the time if it were not important."

  Notice how contractions create a conversational style.

  "If you're going to be in town, let's meet Monday morning. I wouldn't ask you to take the time if it weren't important."

After you write an e-mail message, read through it to "hear" how it sounds. If it reads like an academic thesis or a bureaucratic manual, revise it and loosen up the style. Otherwise, it may put the reader to sleep. Or they'll quickly click "Delete."

Writing Skills

E-mail is fast becoming the most common way businesspeople communicate day to day. But it hasn't replaced and probably won't replace standard documents: written reports, proposals, performance reviews, grant fund applications, business plans, and, yes, even the traditional business letter printed on paper.

Some e-mail users take a too casual approach. Their style of writing isn't conversational; it's careless. And careless writing can damage your credibility. Careless writing can also become a habit. If you write carelessly when you compose e-mail mes-

---

Use Contractions Correctly

⚠️ CAUTION!

Take care not to confuse the contracted form of a word with the possessive form. Mistakes are commonly made with these words, which a spell-check feature won't catch.

- *It's* is the contraction for *it is*, as in "It's going to be a long meeting."
  Its is the possessive form, as in "The company had its annual meeting."
- *You're* is the contraction for *you are*, as in "You're right."
  Your is possessive, as in "Your briefcase is on your desk."
- *They're* is the contraction for *they are*, as in "They're going to be on time."
  Their is possessive, as in "Did you catch their act?"
  There is a direction or location, as in "I'll be there."

sages, before you know it you're writing less carefully in more formal documents.

Good writing makes a good impression. In a well-written message, the meaning is clear. People are less likely to misinterpret. And writing skills continue to be valued in business.

- Use correct spelling, grammar, and punctuation.
- Vary the length of sentences. Well-placed variety creates a rhythmic flow to writing. It improves readability and helps to maintain the reader's interest.
- Refrain from writing run-on sentences. As this sample statement shows, a run-on sentence rambles on and on and so, from the reader's standpoint, it's difficult to follow the writer's train of thought and consequently the meaning you intended may be lost and the reader is frustrated by the time they get to the end of the sentence.
- Use gender-neutral references. Write about businesspeople (not businessmen or businesswomen), police officers, mail carriers, sales agents, and the like.
- Be equitable with masculine and feminine pronouns. At one time, writers took care to refer to both *he* or *she, his* or *her*. It's now considered stilted and distracting to construct a sentence like this: "An executive shows his or her leadership skill." Rewrite the sentence in the plural form: "Executives show their leadership skill." Or drop the problematic adjective: "An executive shows leadership skill."

With a conversational style of writing, it's also now acceptable to use a plural pronoun to refer to a singular noun. "I asked the employee if they agreed the issue was important." It's how we talk—and how I've written this book.

- Take care to use the word that correctly conveys what you mean. Some words appear and sound similar, but have different meanings. Watch out for words like *accept* and *except, affect* and *effect, credible* and *creditable, ensure* and *insure.*

- Eliminate outdated words and phrases like "pursuant to our agreement" and "please be advised that." Few people, if any, talk that way. It's ineffective to write that way.
- Eliminate unnecessary verbiage. It serves no purpose. And in e-mail messages it takes up space on the screen. It isn't necessary to write, "The purpose of this message is to let you know ..." or "I'm writing to tell you that ...." Just get to the point.

Instead of starting a sentence, "Due to the fact that ...," use "Because ...." A payment "in the amount of $100" is payment "for $100." And "at this point in time" is "now." You don't need to add, "Let me know if you have any questions." If the reader has questions, they'll ask.

- Eliminate redundant expressions. Here are some common examples.
  A *consensus of opinion* is a *consensus.*
  You don't *postpone until later*; you *postpone.*
  It isn't *reduced down*; it's *reduced.*
  Replace *shuttled back and forth* with *shuttled.*
  It's not *adequate enough*; it's either *adequate* or *enough.*
- Watch out for misplaced modifiers. An error that's often overlooked, a misplaced modifier can alter the meaning of a sentence. What does this sentence tell you?
  "Since they were rowdy in the company meeting, the managers excused the employees from the shipping department." Who was rowdy?
  The modifying phrase, "Since they were rowdy," was intended to refer to "employees." But the placement suggests it was the managers who were rowdy.
  To prevent confusion or misinterpretation, place modifying words or phrases nearest the noun they're meant to modify. In this example, rearrange the sentence:
  "Since they were rowdy in the company meeting, the employees from the shipping department were excused."

"The managers excused the employees from the shipping department because they were rowdy in the company meeting."

"Since the employees from the shipping department were rowdy in the company meeting, the managers excused them."

- Proofread. Speed is one of the reasons e-mail's so popular. Messages are transmitted in the blink of an eye. In a rush to get off an e-mail, sometimes we write hurriedly.

  Hasty writing can result in errors. Before you press "Send," pause long enough to proofread. For long messages, you may find it easier to proofread printed copy.

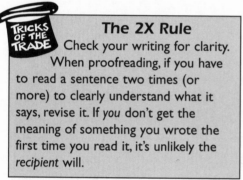

The 2X Rule

Check your writing for clarity. When proofreading, if you have to read a sentence two times (or more) to clearly understand what it says, revise it. If *you* don't get the meaning of something you wrote the first time you read it, it's unlikely the *recipient* will.

Replying to E-Mail

E-mail users perceive that the moment they press "Send," their messages are delivered. So they're expectant, waiting for a reply. But a message delivered is not a message read—not until the recipient picks it up. Even then, a lot of time may pass between reading and replying.

Being slow to respond defeats, in part, the purpose of e-mail. Check your e-mail at least twice a day, at the beginning and end of each work day. Reply promptly to messages that pertain to business.

When a sender requests information and you don't have it yet, reply immediately to acknowledge receipt of their request. Let the sender know when you'll get back to them with the information. If you don't acknowledge the initial message, some users grow impatient and send another one.

When using the "Reply" option to respond to a sender's message, follow these guidelines.

- Leave the subject line of the original message as is. Don't change it. Since it's the subject the sender has in mind, it's what they'll look for to identify your reply.
- To headline a key point of your reply, use a "Re: " line at the top of the text area.
- If you have only a partial response, send that. Let the person know when to expect the rest. For example:
  From sender: <u>Subject: Schedule for System Conversion</u>
  Your reply: Re: Phase I
  Marty,
  The attachment SYSTESTS outlines our schedule for test runs in Phase I.
  You'll have the Phase II schedule by Wednesday, 9/17.

- Put your reply ahead of the original message received from the sender. (Your e-mail program may do this automatically.) Never write your reply within the body of the sender's text.

- Stick to the subject of the original message. If you have something to say to the sender on another subject, put it in a separate message.

E-Mail Policies

Here's the most important thing to know about an e-mail policy. Have one.

Some people are opposed to a written policy. But experts in employment law caution: it's foolhardy and potentially costly not to have an e-mail policy.

According to L. Camille Hebert, professor in The Ohio State University College of Law, "E-mail messages sent by supervisors and other employees may provide an employee with valuable evidence of discriminatory intent or other wrongful conduct."

Employment specialist Daniel Weisberg, a partner in the law firm of Brobeck, Phleger & Harrison, adds a related concern. "The most common problem we hear about," he notes, "are employees who are offended by all the sexually explicit e-mail jokes that bounce around these offices."

At the least, an e-mail policy should address the following concerns:

- confidentiality of company information
- the use of copyrighted material
- biased, defamatory, obscene, or harassing content

An e-mail policy should be in writing, reviewed with all employees, and covered with new hires during their orientation. All employees should be asked to sign their agreement to comply with the e-mail policy. Assure employees that the policy offers them protection from receiving undesirable material.

Smart Managing

Research the Resources

Search the Internet for current information about e-mail policies, privacy issues, cyberfraud, spam (junk e-mail), and virus protection. You might also want to subscribe to a few lists that will keep you informed about news in these areas.

Voice Mail

You check your voice-mail messages. Do you sometimes hear messages that sound like this?

> This is Barry. I'm calling from the airport and I think my cell phone battery is running low so I hope you get this message. Need to talk to you about ... uh ... oh, yeah, the meeting next week. I want to be sure we get three things on the agenda. First, the system conversion. Let's get an update from the team leader. Have you talked with her lately? And ... um ... what else? Oh, right: we need to confirm the budget for that project, too. If you need to talk to me about it, call me at the hotel tonight. The number's .... Hold on a sec .... I've got it here somewhere ... xxx-xxx-xxxx. (The telephone number is rattled off so rapidly you can't write fast enough to get it down the first time you listen to this message). OK. That's it for now. Oh, by the way, say hello to Sam when you see him at the awards banquet. Lemme see ... um .... One more

thing for the meeting. Check with Sandy in the training department and see if she can do a 10-minute presentation on using voice mail. I've been hearing a lot of complaints from employees about our system. (Click.)

Like e-mail, voice mail is intended to be a convenience. But it's convenient only if people use it effectively.

Leaving a Message

To be effective on the phone, follow these six simple steps.

1. Before you place a call, have in mind what you're going to say. Make it easy for people to listen to you. Communicate a well-organized message.

   You might find it helpful to first write down a few key word notes of the points you want to be sure to cover. To make it easy on the listener, talk through them in a logical, progressive order.
2. Begin by saying who's calling. Give your first and last names. Even if you're leaving a message for someone you've talked to numerous times, don't assume they'll recognize your voice. They may talk to hundreds of people during a week and you may sound similar to someone else.
3. State the reason for your call in one brief sentence. Confine each message to one subject in case the recipient wants to forward the message to someone else.
4. Specify what you need. If you want a call back, give at least two times when you can be reached. If you need information, state specifically *what* you need, *when* you need it, *how* it should be sent, and *where* to send it.

   When you give your telephone number, e-mail address, fax number, and/or mailing address, speak clearly and slowly. Typically, people jot down notes while listening. It's time-consuming and annoying to have to rewind a message, sometimes several times, in order to get down what the caller said.

   If you've called to give the listener information, indicate if you need a response or not. Say something like "Please confirm that you've received this" or "I don't need a call back unless there's something you want me to clarify."

For sales calls, make your message of interest to the listener. Mention two or three benefits that give the listener reason to want to talk with you.

5. Omit idle talk that's unrelated to the subject you've called about. As you do with e-mail, keep your message short and to the point.

6. Speak naturally. Imagine that you're talking to the person face to face. Smile and stand when you talk on the phone. Your voice will project more enthusiasm.

Responding to Messages

Check your voice-mail messages on a regular basis, at least twice during the work day: morning and afternoon. Respond to messages promptly. A person who doesn't return phone calls earns a reputation for being discourteous.

You'll also get more calls. If a caller leaves a message today and doesn't hear back from you, they'll call again in a couple of days. And again ... and again.

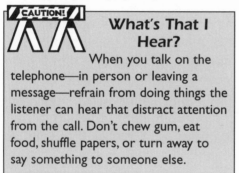

What's That I Hear?
When you talk on the telephone—in person or leaving a message—refrain from doing things the listener can hear that distract attention from the call. Don't chew gum, eat food, shuffle papers, or turn away to say something to someone else.

Faxes

As e-mail use has increased, fax use has declined. But there are still applications for fax communications. Fax is popular for sending order forms and multi-page documents that may not transmit well (or at all) via e-mail between incompatible systems. And some users still prefer fax over e-mail.

When you send a fax, apply these pointers.

• Check the quality and legibility of the document. High-contrast images fax far better than colors and shades of gray. Black print on a white background is clearest.

- If you want your transmission to get immediate attention, first make a courtesy call to the recipient. Alert them to an incoming fax.
- Conserve on paper. If you're sending a message that will fit on one page, put the "To/From" information in a boxed header at the top of the page. Add your message below that. There's no need to use a separate cover sheet that shows "FAX" spelled out in 96-point type across the top.

The Communicator's Checklist for Chapter 9

❏ Use the form of communication most likely to get you the response you want when you need it.

❏ Whether writing or calling, identify five fundamental factors: who, what, when, where, and why.

❏ Using a conversational style of writing. Compose and format e-mail messages for optimum readability.

❏ Establish an e-mail policy in writing.

❏ Before making a telephone call, organize your thoughts. When leaving a voice-mail message, speak clearly and stick to the point.

Finishing
Touches

Easy communication, the absence of barriers to talking to one
another are essential.
— a senior manager quoted in *In Search of Excellence*

S oon after it was published in 1982, *In Search of Excellence*
became a best-seller. In it, authors Tom Peters and Robert
Waterman, Jr. described the attributes of excellent companies.
Achieving excellence became the theme of corporate conferences and the topic of discussion among business leaders and
managers.

Since the book first captivated business-minded readers,
much has changed. Many organizations have restructured, shifting from "old order" hierarchies to flatter and freer forms.
Technology has advanced. Telecommuting has increased. E-
commerce and dot.com companies have come on the scene.

But some things haven't changed: human nature and the
need to interact effectively. To achieve excellence—as a manager and as an organization—interpersonal skills are essential. The
additional pointers in this final chapter help, too.

Communicating with the Boss

Every business and working relationship you have has the potential to contribute to your success. Few are more instrumental than your relationship with your boss. This is the person who weighs your ideas, evaluates your performance, approves your next pay raise, and influences your promotability within the organization. Handle with care.

Know the Boss's Goals

Some bosses clearly convey their goals and objectives to their managers. Others don't. It's not that a boss intentionally withholds such information. Usually, it's an oversight or they assume you know the goals they have in mind, even if they haven't spelled them out.

If you don't know your boss's goals, find out. Initiate a discussion on the subject and ask. "As the manager of _____, I want to support you in reaching your goals. What do you want to achieve?"

Because circumstances change, periodically revisit the issue. At least quarterly, ask for an update so you'll know if the goals have changed. Direct your efforts and steer your department accordingly.

When you report on results, communicate in terms that relate specifically to the boss's goals. "From these midyear figures, you can see we're better than halfway to the goal you want to reach by year end."

Show Your Support

Disagreements are bound to happen. They can be healthy for an organization (provided they don't degenerate into unresolved conflicts). Differences of

---

WIIFT

Zig Ziglar has made a career of writing and speaking about what motivates people. He suggests that we're all tuned in to the same radio station. Its call letters are WIIFM, meaning What's In It For Me? When you communicate with your boss—to propose an idea, report results, request resources—describe WIIFT, meaning What's In It For Them? You improve your odds of gaining approval when you make clear the advantages the boss stands to gain.

opinion can spur discussions that lead to better understanding, fresh ideas, and solutions to mutual concerns. In fact, as management consultant and best-selling author Kenneth Blanchard points out, in paraphrasing William Wrigley, when two people always agree, one of them isn't necessary.

You may not always agree with your boss. You may not approve of every decision that comes down from the boss or other higher-ups. But never express your disagreement in the presence of employees. If you do, employees won't give the decision their full support because they rightly perceive that management is splintered over the issue. And your boss may conclude that you're disloyal.

Drawing the Line on Loyalty to the Boss

In most situations, convey to employees that you're in concert with your boss and higher-ups. There's one exception: if a boss engages in conduct that is illegal, immoral, or unethical. There, draw the line. In a case of conflicting loyalties, loyalty to the well-being of the organization overall or to your own convictions takes precedence over blind loyalty to a boss.

When you're responsible for implementing a decision you don't agree with, tell employees, "The company has decided _____ for these reasons." Explain the rationale behind the decision, emphasizing the benefits. Add, "I'm giving this decision my full support, and I count on you to support it, too."

Ask for Feedback

Chapter 5 pointed out that many managers find it difficult to give corrective feedback. Uneasy about facing up to performance problems, they allow an employee to continue a behavior they wish the employee would correct. What if *you* are that employee?

If your boss is reluctant to give you feedback, you're not getting the benefit of input to improve your performance on an ongoing basis. Your boss may have expectations you haven't been told about and so can't fulfill. Your boss may be bothered by something that you could correct if you were aware of it.

Make it easy on your boss. If your boss seems reluctant to give feedback, ask for it.

Look for opportune times to raise the issue. When your boss delegates an assignment to you, say something like "This is similar to the assignment I did last month. Is there anything you'd like me to do better this time?" If you present quarterly reports to the boss, when you're finished say, "This next quarter, I want to continue to improve my management skills. What would you suggest I do?"

When your boss gives you feedback, receive it agreeably. Don't make excuses. Don't react defensively. Do what you wish your employees would do when you give them feedback. Be receptive and act on it. Learn the skills or take the steps to make the improvements your boss mentions.

If you have aspirations to move ahead in the organization, let your boss know. Ask, "Specifically, what do I need to do to advance in my career?" Then do it.

Adapt to Your Boss

Zack prizes collaboration and frequent communication. He takes pride in paying careful attention to detail. Most mornings, he drops by the boss's office to report on the previous day's activities and get his boss's input.

During a discussion of his performance, Zack is surprised by his boss's remarks, "You need to act on your own initiative more" and "You don't see the big picture." Neither assessment is true, in fact. But Zack's boss formed those perceptions because she's an empowering leader. She delegates responsibility, expects managers to make their own decisions, and prefers to be briefed only when a problem occurs.

Jan is a "take-charge" type of manager. She figures the department's her responsibility. She doesn't want to bother her boss with details she considers inconsequential. When her department meets or exceeds goals, Jan sends the boss a casual e-mail message.

During a discussion of her performance, Jan is surprised by the boss's remarks, "You neglect to keep me informed" and

"You lack business writing skills." Neither assessment is true, in fact. But Jan's boss formed those perceptions because he's a micro-manager. He prefers detailed reports on a regular basis and in the form of a printed document.

These scenarios illustrate how misperceptions can form when your management and communication styles don't coincide with your boss's.

When it comes to interacting with you and being kept informed, what does your boss prefer? Checkmark his or her preferences.

Style

❑ Formal meetings
❑ Informal chats, wherever you happen to meet: in the hallway, break room, parking lot
❑ Conversations in the privacy of the boss's office
❑ Detailed reports in writing
❑ Typed memos summarizing key points
❑ Handwritten notes left on the boss's desk
❑ E-mail messages

Frequency

❑ Daily briefings
❑ Weekly updates
❑ Only "as needed," when a special situation arises or a problem occurs

If you don't know your boss's preferences, ask. For a favorable working relationship, adapt your methods and frequency of communication to the boss's style and preferences.

Communicating with Your Peers

Mark, Marta, and Matt manage different departments in the same organization and work in the same building.

On their way out to lunch one day, Mark and Matt stop by Marta's office and invite her to join them. Seated in front of her computer, she looks up from her work long enough to say, "Not today. I'm busy." The next three times they invite her, she gives them the same answer. They stop asking.

Traveling together to a trade show, the three are waiting in the boarding area at the airline terminal. While Matt and Mark carry on a conversation, Marta makes calls on her cell phone. During the trade show, Matt and Mark arrange to meet for dinner. They ask Marta if she wants to go. "Can't," she tells them. "I have work to do." She goes to her hotel room and plugs in her laptop computer.

The next week, employees in Marta's department are rushing to finish a project. Marta heads across the hall and asks Mark, "Can I borrow Roy this afternoon? I need some extra help to make this deadline." "Sorry," Mark says. "Roy's got a full workload here." Later in the day, Marta notices Roy working in Matt's department.

If Marta's insightful, she'll learn from this incident a useful lesson. Don't overlook the importance of building bridges of good working relationships with your peers.

Picture your network of interpersonal communications as shown in Figure 10-1.

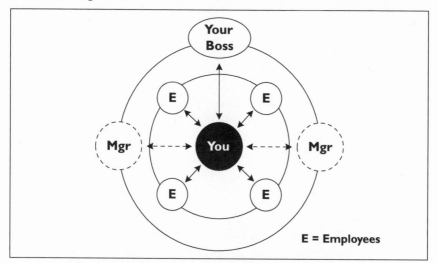

Figure 10-1. A network of interpersonal communications

It consists of circles of influence and input. Whenever you interact with others, you influence them: their perceptions, opinions, sometimes their performance, and always how they respond to you. You receive input from them, sometimes valuable information and ideas. Your immediate circle involves the employees you manage. The outer circle extends to your boss—and should include your peers.

Use your communication skills to build alliances with your fellow managers. Interact with them on a regular basis. From among your peers, identify those who fill the following roles.

- *Brainstorming partners*: stimulate your thinking and engage in a lively exchange of ideas. They're creative thinkers and problem solvers.
- *Supporters*: offer encouragement and, when asked, kindly advice. You can count on them to back you up and add their support to ideas you propose.
- *Critics*: serve as "sounding boards" and play the role of devil's advocate. A critic will pick apart ideas and pose the tough questions that prompt you to more carefully examine your thinking.

To protect our fragile egos, we tend to avoid critics. But their analytical, sometimes skeptical view serves a useful purpose. From a critic's input, you may realize that your "good idea" isn't such a good idea after all. Or you'll refine the idea to make it better—*before* you present it to employees or propose it to the boss.

In return for what your peers do for you, which roles do you fill for them?

Smart Managing

Iron Sharpens Iron

Proverbs 27:17 attests to the value of interacting with your peers: "As iron sharpens iron, so one man sharpens another." This mutual sharpening produces synergy—the energy of a system. When individuals work together as a "system," the resulting energy is greater than the sum of its parts.

From interactions with your peers, you gain individually. An informal network of peer exchange also produces a stronger management team, which adds strength to the business unit overall.

Connect to the Grapevine

Take another look at the diagram of your network of interpersonal communications (Figure 10-1). Picture

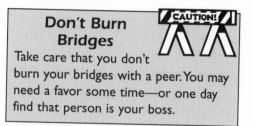

Don't Burn Bridges

Take care that you don't burn your bridges with a peer. You may need a favor some time—or one day find that person is your boss.

it duplicated for every work group in the organization. There's another network of communications winding throughout these work groups. It's informal and lightning-fast: the grapevine.

Every organization has one. It's a channel of information that gets fed from hallway chats, conversations carried on in the break room, remarks made in elevators, comments made in the parking lot and passed on through e-mail. It's not unusual for employees connected to the grapevine to get news before you do.

You learn a lot by tapping into the grapevine and keep better abreast of what's going on. What are employees talking about? What's on their minds? What has their attention? What's bothering them? What seeds of rumor or gossip are being sown that ought to be nipped in the bud before they take on a life of their own? A fiction often becomes a fact by the time it progresses halfway through the grapevine.

How do you tap the grapevine? First, be approachable and trustworthy. When you are, employees are more inclined to come to you with something they've heard through the grapevine. They'll check it out with you first, before they spread it further.

Hang around. Get out of your office or cubicle, out from behind your desk, and mingle with the "troops." Join groups in the break room. If you're putting into practice the constructive communication skills we've discussed, you'll be welcome.

Occasionally, ask two or three employees to join you for lunch. Over time, include every employee so you're not seen as playing favorites or excluding anyone. Take part in after-hours activities, like the company softball team.

Does your department or business unit produce a newsletter? Read it. And encourage employees to contribute columns or "Letters to the Editor." The issues employees write about sometimes reflect what's running through the grapevine.

When you join employees to connect to the grapevine, assume a passive role. Listen. Don't react to things you hear. Don't add your comments to the grapevine. If you do, they'll get distorted down the line. And never use anything you hear against someone. If you do, that'll get known through the grapevine, too, and your connection will be cut off.

Communicate Through Change

Few things fly through the grapevine faster than word of a change.

When a change occurs, the greater its impact on employees, the more crucial your interpersonal skills become. Every communication is important: the presentation you give announcing the change, the meetings you lead to discuss implementation, the corrective feedback you give the employee who chronically complains about the change.

It's commonly said that people resist change. That's a sweeping and inaccurate generalization. Not everyone resists change, especially nowadays, when change is so commonplace we've come to expect it.

You'll notice people exhibit various attitudes toward change.

- *Innovative.* These are people who initiate changes they consider improvements.
- *Receptive.* These people welcome a change when they know and accept the benefits it can bring.
- *Resigned.* These folks gradually go along with the change because they don't think they have any options.
- *Resistant.* People fight a change when they don't know what to expect and fear the worst. Resistance is an expression of "fear of the unknown."

To reduce resistance, make known "the unknown."

Some managers are reluctant to mention that a change is expected until they have all the facts. Others don't want to deliver "bad news." But you owe it to employees to help them prepare for a change that's going to affect them. It's a matter of trust.

If you're slow to tell employees about an upcoming change, they'll hear rumblings about it from the rumor mill. And we all know what the rumor mill does: it distorts the facts and fuels fears. When employees hear about a change from a source other than you, not only do you lose their trust, but you also risk losing control of the situation.

Communicate Early and Often

As soon as you become aware of a forthcoming change, announce it to employees. Be candid. Express the anticipated benefits, but don't oversell them. And don't underplay the adjustments people may have to make as they go through the transition from "old" to "new."

If you don't have all of the details yet, let employees know what you do know. Tell them things are still in the planning stages. Offer reassurance that you'll keep them posted as the change progresses.

Keep the topic of the change open to discussion. If you don't, some employees will conclude you're hiding something. If employees suspect you're keeping secrets, they'll feel they have reason to fear—which raises resistance.

Keep employees apprised of what's going on. From one meeting or discussion to the next, don't let too many

Change Raises Questions

When a change occurs, employees want to know:

Smart
Managing

1. What's happening?
2. Where is this taking us?
3. How are we going to make it work?
4. How will it affect me?

Be prepared to answer their questions. On the third one—How are we going to make it work?—involve employees in the answer. Welcome their suggestions. So they don't see themselves as passive "victims" of a change in which they have no say, help them take ownership of it. Assign employees active roles in carrying out the transition.

weeks go by without communicating something about the status of the change. Even an e-mail to say that nothing new has happened will help put people's minds at ease. If you don't give employees updates on a regular basis, one or two will start to use their imaginations and crank up the rumor mill.

Use Values and Evaluations

One constant you can count on is that little will remain the same. Something will change. Expect it. And expect that some employees may react unfavorably when a change occurs.

Prepare to deal with such reactions by having in place these two things.

1. Organizational values stated in writing
2. A written job description or performance plan for each employee—including a statement that reads, "Employees are expected to support the organization's values."

When a change occurs, if an employee balks at it or bad-mouths it, point out how the change is related to the organization's values. Reiterate the expectation that employees support those values and, by extension, support the change.

Take the case of the Automated Billing Company. It values:

- Quality
- Reliability
- Exceptional customer service
- Profitability

The manager of the client service department announced the company was changing to a new computer system. The manager explained the change in terms of the company's values: the new system will speed response time, which will improve customer service, and the new technology is more reliable.

If an employee resists the change, the manager is prepared to give corrective feedback based on the expectation stated in the job description.

Communicate Through Stories

When Nordstrom expanded and opened department stores in California, a customer went to one of the new stores to return a set of tires. Nordstrom doesn't sell tires. But the customer insisted he'd bought them at a Nordstrom store. Eager to satisfy the customer, a store employee took the tires and gave the customer a credit. Or so the story goes.

Have you heard the one about basketball coach Larry Bird? He expects his players to be on time. On one occasion, two players were late for the scheduled departure of a charter flight taking the team to an out-of-town game. Coach Bird directed the pilot to take off without them. Or so the story goes.

Herman Miller, Inc. is a leading furniture manufacturing company. Max DePree, chairman of the board, stopped by a tennis club to play a few matches with a friend. Entering the locker room after a group of high school students had been there, he noticed they'd left towels lying around. DePree picked up the towels and tossed them in a hamper. His friend asked if he picked up towels because he was president of a company or was he president of a company because he picked up towels? Or so the story goes.

These three stories very effectively convey a sense of values and beliefs. They show values and beliefs in action, put into practice.

David M. Boje is a professor of management at New Mexico State University, editor of the *Journal of Organizational Change Management,* and an expert on storytelling in organizations. According to Boje, "3M, HP, IBM, DuPont, Kimberly-Clark, Patagonia, Disney, Nike and other corporations are looking to storytelling to make their business plans and strategies more compelling."

A well-crafted, well-told story is compelling. It touches people at an emotional level—and it's emotion that motivates. People aren't driven to achieve and excel because of facts; they're driven by how they feel. As Stephen Maloney, an executive with Aetna Life & Casualty, observed, "Many business people deny it, but businesses are really run on emotion."

In addition to its emotional appeal, a good story does something equally important. If I tell you a story that expresses an aspect of your own experience, we share a mutual understanding. The story creates between us one of the essentials of constructive communication: commonality. It produces what communication aims for: shared understanding.

Stories can impress upon people "lessons" you want them to learn, without sounding like you're lecturing at them. No one likes lectures. And a good story will be remembered long after a lecture's been forgotten. What's the lesson in the Nordstrom story? In the story about Coach Bird? What's the lesson in the story of a chief executive picking up sweat-stained towels from a locker room floor?

Stories that circulate within the organization can convey values. They can serve to orient new hires to the corporate culture. For individuals and work groups, a compelling story can illustrate the meaning in their jobs or renew a sense of purpose.

When a story circulates outside of the organization, it has the power to shape public perceptions. Companies like Southwest Airlines, FedEx, and Nordstrom (to name a few) have gained great benefit from stories told about their customer service.

To have positive impact, a story must be well constructed and well told. A good story:

- speaks to the audience, causing listeners to relate to it
- makes a point
- stirs emotion or provokes thought
- entertains, amuses, or inspires
- is communicated expressively
- is brief

What stories are told in your organization? What messages and meanings do they convey? How do *you* use stories: in meetings, presentations, and one-on-one conversations? How

Sources for Storytelling

Unless you're a skilled storyteller, don't attempt to pull off a potentially high-impact story without preparation and practice. Telling a story well is like telling a joke: it takes timing and inflection.

• Search your local library or the Internet for publications about organizational storytelling. On the Internet, David M. Boje's home page is worth checking out: http://cbae.nmsu.edu/~dboje/

• Read the autobiographies of business leaders, military heroes, or sports stars. Read business publications that feature profiles of success stories.

• Listen to professional speakers. Most have developed good storytelling techniques. You can hear them at conferences, in seminars, and on audio and video tapes.

could you use stories to make a greater impact when you communicate?

Communicate with Humor

In an area of average-priced homes, a real estate agent who consistently produces multimillion dollar sales figures attributes much of his success to a sense of humor. Dave Sawyer has found, "If you have a good relationship and can talk and laugh, you can give people good news or bad news equally the same."

In recent years, organizations have begun to recognize the value of humor. Companies considered to be on the conservative side—AT & T, Deloitte & Touche, General Motors, IBM, Monsanto, Xerox—have hired humor consultants to show them how to lighten up.

A more contemporary company, ice-cream maker Ben & Jerry's, has incorporated humor into its corporate culture since its inception. The position that oversees internal communications carries with it the refreshing title "The Grand Poobah of Joy." And at Southwest Airlines, CEO Herb Kelleher counts a sense of humor among the qualities his company looks for when hiring.

Research has discovered numerous benefits to humor. Here's what laughter can do for you:

- It raises morale.
- It boosts productivity.
- It speeds problem solving.
- It relieves stress.
- It eases tensions.
- It counteracts negativity.
- It improves customer service.

Many of these benefits contribute to improved interactions. When, for example, employees are less stressed, they're less likely to react. They're more likely to respond reasonably when dealing with one another or when dealing with you. When morale is high, fewer conflicts occur. Humor and laughter are communication cues that put people at ease. They make us more receptive to hearing what the other person has to say.

For all its benefits, there are forms of humor that are not appropriate in the workplace. Avoid anything that's in poor taste or insensitive of others. Laugh *with* people, never *at* them. If anyone is the object of humor, make it you; never poke fun at someone else. Keep the humor clean and good-natured for everyone involved.

Most work groups have at least one or two employees who are naturally humorous. You may be one of those people. If so,

Making Humor Happen

When I was walking down the hallway of a company I was visiting for a meeting, a closed office door caught my attention. Top to bottom, it was covered with cartoons, comic strips, and humorous quotes. I stopped and read and laughed and read and laughed. That door was a day-brightener.

On another occasion, I was sitting in a lobby waiting for an appointment. Every few minutes, one of the office staff came out to pick up messages from the receptionist. Each person was dressed in costume—and it wasn't Halloween. Naturally, I was curious and asked the receptionist about it. She explained, "You know how some companies have Casual Friday? We have a once-a-month Dress-Up Day."

For ideas on how you can introduce more humor into your work place, check out The Humor Project at http://www.humorproject.com.

you probably already have employees laughing. If not, acknowledge those who are humorous. When they make an amusing remark at a meeting, join in the laughter. Welcome their ideas on how to "lighten up" the atmosphere. Ask them to head up a "Humor Huddle"—a small group charged with coming up with ways to make the workplace more fun.

According to humor consultant Patty Wooten, author of *Compassionate Laughter: Jest for Your Health*, "If management ain't laughing, ain't nobody laughing." If nobody's laughing, nobody's finding much enjoyment in their jobs. Have you noticed? People give their best efforts to jobs they enjoy.

Communicate Through MBM

The practice of management evolves. As with most things, it goes through changes over time.

During the 1980s, the popular approach to management was MBO: Management by Objectives. During the 1990s, MBWA—Management by Walking Around—came into vogue. Although it's not effective with employees, some managers persist in practicing the "old order" style of MBHH: Management by Hovering and Hounding.

A contemporary approach is MBM: Management by Modeling. It's based on the premise that when you're in a position of leadership—be it first-line supervisor or chief executive—you're a behavioral model. Employees look up to you and take cues from you.

Model Bridge Building

MBM recognizes the influence of communications—both verbal and nonverbal. Verbally you say, "Here's what I need you to do to improve your performance." Visually (by your behavior) you convey, "Here's what it looks like."

Consider this question: What do I want employees to do when they interact with one another? when they interact with me? Here are three answers I've heard from countless managers: "I wish employees would ..."

- *Listen.* If you want employees to listen to you, you need to listen to them. Be a model of attentive listening.
- *Take corrective feedback without getting defensive.* You need to lead the way. Ask employees for their feedback about your performance as their manager. Show that you're receptive to what they have to say. Don't react defensively; welcome their input and act on it. Model for employees what you want them to do when they get feedback from you.
- *Show a positive attitude.* Exemplify an optimistic outlook yourself. Speak in terms of positive possibilities, options, solutions, and a hopeful future. Let them hear from you how a pleasant, cheerful tone of voice sounds. And by your behavior—a smile on your face, a spring in your step, an enthusiastic approach to the job at hand—model how a positive attitude looks.

The first chapter of this book compared interpersonal communication with bridge building. When you interact—with employees, your boss, or peers—your objective is to build bridges of positive, productive working relationships.

Consistently apply the communication skills we've discussed and you'll be a master bridge builder. You'll be pleased with the results.

The Communicator's Checklist for Chapter 10

❏ Be astute about communicating with your boss and peers.

❏ Tune in to what's *really* going on through the grapevine.

❏ Communicate early and often to ease employees through change.

❏ Enrich your communications with stories and humor.

❏ Manage by modeling.

Index